In Search of History

The Twentieth Century

J.F. Aylett

Hodder & Stoughton

A MEMBER OF THE HODDER HEADLINE GROUP

For Phebe, Diana and Phil

Order: Please contact Bookpoint Ltd, 130 Milton Park, Abingdon, Oxon OX14 4SB. Telephone: (44) 01235 827720. Fax: (44) 01235 400454. Lines are open from 9 am – 6 pm Monday to Saturday, with a 24 hour message answering service. You can also order through our website at www.hodderheadline.co.uk

British Library Cataloguing in Publication Data
In search of history, the twentieth century.
  1. Great Britain, History, 20th Century
  I. Aylett, J. F.
  941'.082

ISBN 0 7131 0688 3

First published 1986
Impression number   20 19 18 17 16 15
Year   2004 2003 2002

Printed in Great Britain for Hodder & Stoughton Educational, a division of Hodder Headline Plc, 338, Euston Road, London NW1 3BH by J. W. Arrowsmith Ltd, Bristol

Acknowledgements

The author wishes to thank the following government departments and other organisations for providing information for this book:
The Department of Employment; The Home Office; the Foreign Office; the Department of Health and Social Security; the Equal Opportunities Commission; the Commonwealth Institute; Plaid Cymru; the Scottish National Party; the Trades Union Congress; the Campaign for Nuclear Disarmament; British Rail; Robert Key MP.

The diagram on page 38 is based on a similar diagram in *Benito Mussolini and Fascist Italy*, (Links series) by Robert Wolfson (Edward Arnold 1984).

The publishers would like to thank the following for their permission to reproduce copyright photographs: John Frost: pp 4 t & b, 35b, 47; Popperfoto: pp 5b, 12, 59 l & r, 61; Labour Party Library: pp 5t, 37t (Donna Thynne), 56 (John Chapman); The Mansell Collection Ltd: pp 7t, 9, 48, 55t, 85 l; Bradford Central Library: p 10; BBC Hulton Picture Library: pp 11 l, 26, 29, 31 t & b, 40r, 45, 69; Punch: pp 11r, 49; The *Illustrated London News* Picture Library: p 14; The Museum of London/Donna Thynne: p 15 l & r; Imperial War Museum: pp 19, 21 l, 40 l, 66; *Evening Echo*, Basildon: p 21r; London Express News and Feature Services: pp 23, 57r; Wellcome Institute: p 24; Family Planning Association: p 25b; Science Museum Library: p 25t; TUC Library: p 27 l (text); Ford Motor Co. Ltd: p 33 (inset); British Airways/RAF Museum: p 34; The British Newspaper Library, Colindale: p 37b, 39; British Rail/OPC Railprint: p 51; BT Batsford Ltd: p 52b; GLC Photograph Library: pp 52t, 53; Inner London Education Authority: p 55b; Hereford City Library: pp 58 l, 86; Barry Plummer: p 58r; Royal Marines Public Relations Office: p 63; Daisy Hayes: p 64; Photo Source: pp 67, 81 l; COI: p 69; Whitworth Art Gallery, University of Manchester: p 70; Camera Press: pp 71, 81r, 94; Conservative Central Office: pp 72, 92; Ros Asquith: p 73; Syndication International: pp 75, 90; National Museum of Labour History: p 76; Keith Pattison: pp 77; Chapman + Latham: p 82; Philip Micheu: p 83; Charing Cross and Westminster Medical School: p 85r; Ferranti plc: p 88.

The author supplied material on pages: 7b, 19r, 27r (text), 43 (text), 45 (text), 57 l. The picture on page 33 came from *Every Boys Hobby Annual* 1932. Special thanks go to Harland and Wolff plc and the Merseyside Maritime Museum for their help in reproducing the blueprint for the Titanic on page 13.

The Publishers would like to thank Croom Helm Ltd Publishers for permission to include a map from *The Effects of Nuclear War*, redrawn on page 67.

Contents

Introduction

Today, as I begin writing this book, it is pouring with rain. How do I know? I can see the rain through the window. I can stand in the porch and get wet.

How do you know it is raining as I write this page? Because I have told you. You have read about it in this book.

We get most of our knowledge of the past from books. But how did the writers know that what they wrote was true? They must have had reasons for writing it. They must have had some *evidence* to make them believe it.

Perhaps they were actually alive when the event happened. They might even have taken part in it. In this case, their evidence is a primary source. They were actually there. That is how they knew.

But perhaps it happened long before the writer was born, like the Gunpowder Plot. Luckily, some people wrote about it at the time. Their writings are primary sources.

Some people left behind objects which were used at the time, such as Guy Fawkes' lantern. Objects like that are also primary sources.

Some people made pictures. More recently people may have taken photographs or movie films. Reporters may have written about it for their newspapers. These, too, are all primary sources.

Some people told their friends . . . and they told their friends . . . and, later on, somebody wrote about it. This is different. The person who actually wrote about the event was not alive when it happened. So we call this a secondary source.

So we ought to know what happened. You may think it should be easy to find out what happened in the past. All we have to do is read and look at the primary sources. Then we'll know it all.

But it's not as easy as that! By now, you will know that people don't always agree about what happened. Sometimes, writers are biased; sometimes, they forget; and, sometimes, they make mistakes and get things wrong. So we must be careful when we read or look at primary sources.

Look at the two newspaper reports opposite. Each was printed on April 16th 1912, but one of them just had to be wrong. You probably know which one it was.

The problems don't end there. Think back to the first paragraph. How *do* you know that it was raining when I wrote this? You've only got my word for it. I could be a complete liar. I might have been lying on a beach in Spain.

As it happens, I was telling the truth. But there have been many people in history who have lied. Sometimes, no one has found out for years afterwards. Look at this man.

He is Kim Philby and, for many years, he had an important job in British security. Then, in 1963, he turned up in Russia. People found out that, for 30 years, he had also been a Russian spy – while he had pretended to be seeking Russian spies himself!

There's one more big problem. Look at the poster below. It is one of a pair published in 1923. The titles were YESTERDAY – THE TRENCHES and TO-DAY – UNEMPLOYED.

TO-DAY–UNEMPLOYED

PUBLISHED BY THE LABOUR PARTY 33 Eccleston Square London, S.W. & PRINTED BY VINCENT BROOKS DAY & SON LTD 48 Parker St Kingsway London WC;

It shows a poor family, with a coal-mine in the background. Life was hard for many families after the First World War. There were many people out of work. This drawing is a good primary source.

But it is also something else. This poster was published by the Labour Party and, like all political posters, it is propaganda. This means it has been drawn deliberately to make people think or act in a certain way. This picture tries to make people feel sorry for this family. It is trying to influence people's thinking. What do you think it is trying to get people to do?

You will find that many of the questions in this book ask you what you think. Often, there is no one right answer. Historians have to make up their minds on the basis of the evidence.

And we start by looking at Britain at the beginning of the 20th century. . . .

1 Edwardian Britain

It's the same the whole world over,
It's the poor what gets the blame;
It's the rich what gets the pleasure,
Isn't it a bloomin' shame?

invested governess parasol slum
middle class
poverty line

UPPER CLASS   MIDDLE CLASS   LABOURING CLASS

£20+   £3-£20   £2

UPPER CLASS 2%   MIDDLE CLASS 25%   LABOURER 73%

Households of different classes and their weekly income in 1908.

The Rich

The new century opened with a new king of Great Britain. In 1901, Queen Victoria died and her son, Edward, became King Edward VII. The country he ruled was the richest and most powerful in the world. And some of his people were very rich indeed.

These very rich people enjoyed a life of luxury and ease. Most of them owned land or buildings; they also had huge sums of money **invested**. Many did not need to work; they could live off their investments and rents. A few of them became MPs, which was an unpaid job until 1911.

There was not much for their wives to do, either. Their sons went off to boarding school at an early age; their daughters were taught by **governesses**. All the other household tasks were done by servants. Over 1 690 000 women had jobs as servants in 1901.

So the rich were usually free to spend their time enjoying themselves. In summer, they stayed at their London houses for a whole season of entertainment. They entertained each other for tea and at dinner parties; there were dances and visits to the theatre.

In winter, they had holidays abroad and spent weekends at each other's country houses. The men were busy shooting and hunting while the ladies went riding.

There had always been a wide gulf between the rich and the poor. But, in Edwardian times, many people felt that it was growing even wider. More important, the difference in their lives was becoming more obvious, even to the poor.

New popular newspapers, such as the *Daily Mail*, made it possible for the poor to read about the rich and their way of life. At the same time, there were so many new things for the rich to spend their money on.

Luxury goods came from throughout the Empire; there were many recent inventions, such as the telephone and electric light; above all, there was now the motor car. Money could buy so much more than ever before.

What Mrs Beeton thought guests in a rich household should have for breakfast in 1906. The wealthy host earned about £14 a week; the maid earned about £14 a year.

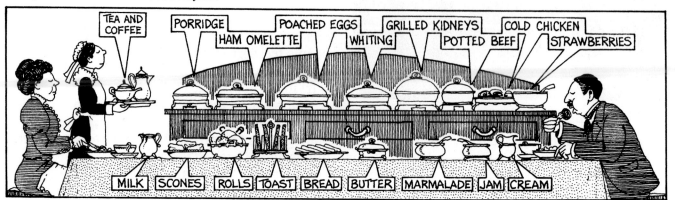

TEA AND COFFEE   PORRIDGE   POACHED EGGS   GRILLED KIDNEYS   COLD CHICKEN
HAM OMELETTE   WHITING   POTTED BEEF   STRAWBERRIES

MILK SCONES ROLLS TOAST BREAD BUTTER MARMALADE JAM CREAM

A C F G Masterman, MP, said in 1909:

We have called into existence a whole new industry in motor cars and quick travelling. We have converted half the Highlands into deer forests for our sport; and the amount annually spent on shooting, racing, golf, exceeds the total [income] of many European [states]. We fling away in elaborate banquets of which one is weary, the price of many poor men's yearly income. Yet we cannot build a new cathedral.

B Marchioness Curzon looked back in 1955:

We went to our first Garden Party in the grounds of Windsor Castle. It remains in my memory as one of the loveliest of the Royal Garden Parties. The ladies of that time dressed beautifully in flowing summer dresses with flower-trimmed hats and lacy **parasols**. They no longer have the time or the leisure to be as beautiful as they were in the early days of this century.

Motoring was not very common then, and the pace of pleasure was far slower than it is to-day. We enjoyed ourselves light-heartedly, and loved every minute of our lives. [Looking back,] the summers seem to have been real summers then – the river always sparkling in the sunlight, the sky always blue.

C Sir Howard Nicolson recalled in 1937:

I do not regret that I was old enough to touch the fringe of Edwardian luxury. But I render thanks that I was also young enough to share the wider liberties of our subsequent age. Let us be frank about it. The Edwardians were vulgar to a degree. They lacked style and it never dawned upon them that intelligence was of any value.

D Cartoon from *The Herald* in October 1914:

SACRIFICE

'Yes, darling, one feels that it is one's duty to set an example of self-denial to the people – I have put Fido and all the dear dogs on the same food as the servants.'

E Fashionable seaside costume (1907):

1 Read the text carefully. Why could poor people not (a) own motor cars; (b) send their sons to boarding schools; (c) visit each other's country houses? Give different reasons for each point.

2 a) Look at the breakfast scene on page 6. Write down the order in which you think these foods were eaten. Give reasons.
b) Which of these foods and drinks do you think the poor could have afforded?

3 a) Read all the written evidence. Which writer is (i) most critical and (ii) least critical of the Edwardian rich?
b) Why do you think that was?
c) Which writer is likely to be least reliable? Explain how you decided.
d) What do writers A and B say about cars?
e) Why are their comments different?
f) Is fashion E for the rich or poor? Explain fully how you decided.

4 a) Look at cartoon D. What is the attitude of the woman towards the poor?
b) What is the cartoonist's attitude towards her? Give reasons for your answer.

A Eel and meat pies for less than 1p!

B Rowntree described life for those who had the bare minimum in 1901:

They must never spend a penny on a railway fare or a bus. They must never go into the country unless they walk. They must never purchase a halfpenny newspaper or spend a penny to buy a ticket for a popular concert. They must write no letters to absent children, for they cannot afford to pay the postage. They must never contribute anything to their church or chapel, or give help to a neighbour which costs them money.

They cannot save, nor can they join sick club or Trade Union, because they cannot afford the contributions. The children must have no pocket money for dolls, marbles or sweets. The father must smoke no tobacco, and must buy no beer. The mother must never buy any pretty clothes for herself or her children. The wage-earner must never be absent from work for a single day.

C Meals for a farm labourer's family in Oxfordshire (1905):

Breakfast – Tea, coffee, bread, sometimes bacon.
Dinner – Boiled bacon, vegetables, tea, sometimes a glass of beer (Sundays – butcher's meat, currant or jam pudding).
Tea – Bread and butter, tea. Sometimes cocoa or coffee.
Supper – Bread, cheese, perhaps a glass of beer (on Sundays, some fresh meat). Most of the men keep pigs. All have gardens or allotments, and many have both. Nearly all the men belong to Benefit Societies, and some to coal and clothing clubs.

The Poor

There is no scientific way of working out whether someone is poor. People may think they are poor even though they are not. The young Winston Churchill once wrote to his mother that they were 'damned poor'. Yet his mother had just spent £200 on a new dress. It would have taken a working man three years to earn that!

However, there are signs which may suggest that someone is poor. One is a lack of food. Another is sickness. A government report in 1904 said that a third of army recruits were rejected because there was something physically wrong with them. Some were seriously ill; others had bad eyesight; many were just too short.

Eleven-year-old town boys were, on average, nearly 4 cms shorter than country boys – and nearly 9 cms shorter than well-off boys at public schools. The army was even forced to reduce its minimum height to 1.5 metres.

These children were shorter mainly because they were poor. Poverty involved:

* not having enough food
* living in overcrowded, **slum** houses
* air pollution
* poorly-educated parents who neglected them

In the 19th century, most people had believed that, if people were poor, it was their fault. By 1900, more and more people disagreed with this.

Some rich people were even studying the poor to find out just what their lives were like. Seebohm Rowntree, of the chocolate family, did a survey in York while Charles Booth, a ship-owner, studied poverty in London.

The evidence section gives some of their findings about the urban poor. Country folk were often worse off. Rowntree wrote about one farm labourer's family in 1913. Mr and Mrs West were bringing up five children on about 60–65p a week. 'But how do you live?' Mrs West was asked.

'I couldn't tell you how we do live; it's a mystery,' she replied. 'I don't know how we manage. The thing is to get it past.'

D Rowntree also described the cycle of life for the poor. He said that, at certain times, they could not help falling below the poverty line:

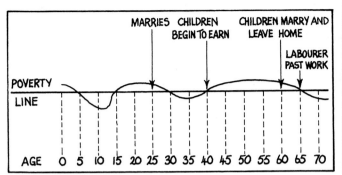

E Weekly budget for a Middlesbrough family (1907):

Mrs A. B.'s Budget
Rent 27½p; coals 11½p; insurance 3p; clothing 5p; meat 7½p; 1 stone of flour 7p; ¼ stone of bread-meal 2p; 1lb butter 5½p; ½lb lard 1p; 1lb bacon 3¾p; 4lb sugar 3¼p; ½lb tea 3¾p; yeast ½p; milk 1¼p; 1 box polish ½p; 1lb soap 1¼p; 1 packet washing powder ½p; 3oz tobacco 3¾p; ½ stone of potatoes 1¼p; onions ½p; matches ½p; lamp oil 1p; debt 1¼p.

F A restaurant gives away its extra food to the poor (1902).

G Growing up in Edwardian times:

I was born in 1899 and started school on my fifth birthday. The school was nearly two miles away, and I had this walk morning and afternoon. In winter, if there was deep snow, a farm wagon took the children from our part of the village to the school. Punishment in the upper classes was severe. There was certainly no vandalism; discipline in the home was always to the fore. If a child was punished at school he or she was punished again at home, either by going to bed supperless or with a taste of dad's strap. It was considered a terrible disgrace for a child to get into trouble at school.

Our food was very plain. We had very little meat, and fish only when a man came round with a covered basket containing a few herrings. This man might come round about twice during the winter months. Our evening meal was often a suet pudding with gravy, or a bread pudding containing currants and spice with a little sugar sprinkled over it. We had half an egg for Sunday breakfast sometimes, when eggs were 16 for 5p. (The men's wages were 50p to 60p a week.) Otherwise we had toast and dripping.

If it was very cold and we were going to school we had kettle tea. This was made with bread broken up and put into a large cup with a lump of dripping, pepper and salt, with boiling water poured on.

Life was quiet and peaceful. We lived in hard times, but being children, we did not fully realise it. We were happy and always busy, my mother's motto being 'Satan finds mischief for idle hands to do'. There was no such thing as being bored as children – we never had time.

1 Explain how each of the following cause poor health: (a) not having enough to eat; (b) air pollution; (c) poor housing; (d) neglect by parents.
   For *each* one, suggest what the government could do to improve the health of the poor.
2 a) In evidence A, what three signs of poverty can you see?
   b) What else could be a sign of poverty? (Use the other evidence to give you ideas.)
3 a) Draw evidence D in your book.
   b) Write down the three times in a lifetime when a person fell below the line. For each time, explain why it happened.

4 a) Read evidence B. What emotion did Rowntree want the reader to feel? Write down the words which he uses to create that emotion.
   b) Would Rowntree have said that the family in E was below the poverty line? Give reasons.
   c) Is the family in E better off than the one in C or not? Explain how you decided.
   d) Work out a typical day's meals for the family in E.
5 a) Read evidence G. Do you think she was poor or not? Give reasons for your answer.
   b) Why does she say they were never bored?
   c) Why do you think many young people today are bored when they live in greater comfort?

2 Help for the Poor

THE GIANT LLOYD-GORGIBUSTER:
Fee, Fi, Fo, Fat,
I smell the blood of a plutocrat;
Be he alive or be he dead,
I'll grind his bones to make my bread.

workhouse National Insurance lentil
on the parish

"FOUR SPECTRES WHICH HAUNT THE POOR"

Lloyd George – and the fears of the poor.

In the 19th century, there were two main political parties in Britain. One was the Conservative Party; the other was the Liberal Party. Neither had done much to help the old, sick or unemployed poor people. They were mostly left to cope by themselves.

Those who could not manage usually wound up living in **workhouses**. These buildings were deliberately made unpleasant so that people would want to get out of them as soon as possible. They were almost a punishment for being poor.

By 1900, many people were beginning to feel that this attitude towards the poor was wrong. One of them was a Liberal politician called Lloyd George. In 1906, the Liberals won a General Election, after years of the Conservatives being in power.

Lloyd George was a leading figure in this new government which began its reforms almost at once. For the first time, a government believed that it must look after those who could not help themselves.

There was plenty of opposition to his ideas. In 1909, the House of Lords objected to his plan to increase taxes. This extra money was partly to pay for his new **National Insurance** scheme.

Doctors objected to it because they were afraid they would lose their independence. And some of the very rich said they would never lick the stamps which it involved. But the Act *was* passed, along with many other plans to help the poor.

Helping the children

A In 1906, the government allowed local councils to provide school meals, with poor children getting a free meal. Bradford was first to offer meals – at a cost of about 1¼p each! This was a week's menu:

Monday **Lentil** and tomato soup. Currant roly-poly pudding.
Tuesday Meat pudding. Rice pudding.
Wednesday Yorkshire pudding, gravy, peas. Rice and sultanas.
Thursday Scotch barley broth. Currant pastry or fruit tart.
Friday Stewed fish, parsley sauce, peas, mashed potatoes. Cornflour blancmange.
All these meals included bread.

B This graph shows how the children gained weight:

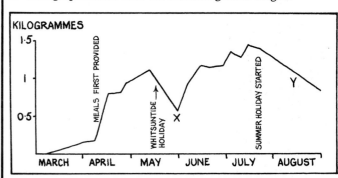

C In the following year, regular medical inspection of all schoolchildren began. Here the headmaster weighs one of the boys:

10

Helping the old

D In 1909, old people in Britain received their first pension. You had to be over 70 and earning less than £31.50 a year to qualify. Amounts varied from 25p to 5p a week, with up to 37½p for a married couple. One pensioner said afterwards:

We was only a burden to our children as kep' us, for they be good and wouldna let us go *on the parish* so long as they could 'elp it. But now we want to go on livin' forever.

Helping the unemployed

In 1910, the first Labour Exchanges opened to help the unemployed find jobs. After 1911, unemployment pay of 35p a week was available to workers in some industries who could not find work.

Helping the sick

E In 1911, all low-paid workers were made to join a new scheme of health insurance. This election poster showed how it worked:

F This cartoon from 1909 shows Lloyd George as Jack the Giant-killer, planning to tax the rich to help pay for the National Insurance scheme:

RICH FARE.

THE GIANT LLOYD-GORGIBUSTER: "FEE, FI, FO, FAT,
I SMELL THE BLOOD OF A PLUTOCRAT;
BE HE ALIVE OR BE HE DEAD,
I'LL GRIND HIS BONES TO MAKE MY BREAD."

1 a) Write each of these dates on a separate line: 1906; 1909; 1910; 1911.
b) Beside each date, write down the reform which took place and who benefited from it.
c) Which reform do you think did most good? Give reasons for your choice.
2 Look carefully at all the evidence. Write down the letters of those you think are biased or propaganda. Explain how you decided.
3 a) Write down *at least* two ways in which menu A is better than the one on page 8 (C).
b) According to evidence B, what was the result of introducing school meals?
c) Why did children lose weight at X and Y?
4 a) Who looked after the pensioner in evidence D before pensions were started?
b) What else could an old person do before 1909 to keep from starving? (*Three* answers.)
5 a) What four benefits did the poster (E) promise insured workers?
b) Lloyd George said the worker was getting '9d for 4d'. What did he mean?
6 Design your own poster to advertise Old Age Pensions. It should be good propaganda, to persuade people that it's a wonderful idea.

3 The *Titanic*

Be British! was the cry as the ship went down,
Ev'ry man was steady at his post,
Captain, and crew, when they knew the worst:
Saving the women and children first.

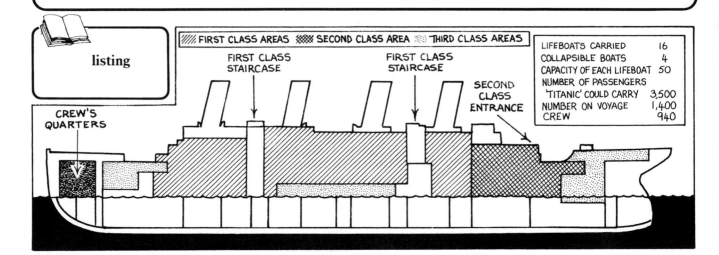

listing

FIRST CLASS AREAS   SECOND CLASS AREA   THIRD CLASS AREAS

FIRST CLASS STAIRCASE   FIRST CLASS STAIRCASE

SECOND CLASS ENTRANCE

CREW'S QUARTERS

LIFEBOATS CARRIED	16
COLLAPSIBLE BOATS	4
CAPACITY OF EACH LIFEBOAT	50
NUMBER OF PASSENGERS 'TITANIC' COULD CARRY	3,500
NUMBER ON VOYAGE	1,400
CREW	940

On Wednesday, April 10th 1912, a ship set out from Southampton, heading for New York. On deck, the band was playing; on the dockside, the crowd cheered and waved.

There was nothing unusual in that. Ships regularly left the port on the Atlantic run. But this ship was special. She was on her first voyage. She was called the *Titanic*.

Everything about the *Titanic* was on a grand scale. She was the biggest ship of her time – and offered the greatest luxury. Apart from the usual accommodation, the *Titanic* had Turkish and electric baths, a gymnasium and a racquet court. One voyage could cost up to £870.

The *Titanic* also offered something else. Her owners said the way she was built made her 'practically unsinkable'. 'God himself,' said one deck-hand, 'could not sink this ship'.

The ice in the Atlantic was further south than

usual that April. Captain Smith of the *Titanic* was radioed more than one warning of icebergs ahead.

By the evening of April 14th, the temperature had dropped below O °C. At 9.20 p.m., the captain left the bridge to get some rest. The lookouts were told to watch for icebergs but the ship sailed on at over 20 knots an hour, close to its top speed.

At 11.35 p.m., the ship hit an iceberg, although most people did not realise it. The emergency doors were closed; the engines were stopped. But the iceberg had damaged the side of the ship. Metal plates had buckled and water was rushing in.

In the wireless cabin, the operator began calling for help. At about 12.25 a.m., lifeboats were lowered. The order was 'Women and Children First'. Many early boats had places to spare; many passengers thought it was safer to stay on the ship. The panic came later. By then, the ship was **listing** badly and it was difficult to lower the boats.

It took just 2½ hours for the *Titanic* to sink; more than 1500 people died. A nearby ship, the *Californian*, had turned off her wireless minutes before the SOS went out. Its captain was afterwards blamed for not going to help but there was probably another ship even nearer which did nothing.

The loss of the *Titanic* brought major changes. After 1913, all ships had to have:
* lifeboat places for everyone on board
* lifeboat drills on every voyage
* a wireless operated 24 hours a day

A photograph taken *during* the voyage. (The passenger got off at Queenstown in Ireland.)

A The *original* blueprint for the *Titanic* showing the number of lifeboats planned:

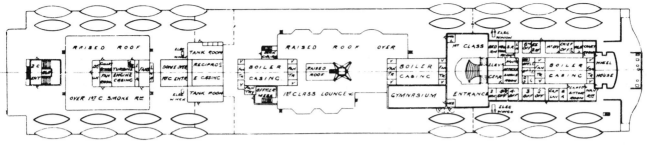

B Casualty figures issued by the Board of Trade:

	First Class			Second Class			Third Class			Total Passengers and Crew		
	Carried	Saved	Per cent Saved	Carried	Saved	Per cent Saved	Carried	Saved	Per Cent Saved	Carried	Saved	Per Cent Saved
Men	173	58	34	160	13	8	454	55	12	1,662	315	19
Women	144	139	97	93	78	84	179	98	55	439	336	77
Children	5	5	100	24	24	100	76	23	30	105	52	49
Total	322	202	63	277	115	42	709	176	25	2,206	703	32

C Harold Bride, second wireless officer, told a reporter after the accident:

'Send a call for assistance,' ordered the captain.

Phillips began to send the 'C.Q.D.' [the old signal, meaning 'Come Quick, Danger']. We joked while he did so. All of us made light of the disaster. We joked that way while he flashed signals for about five minutes. Then the captain came back.

'What are you sending?' he asked. 'C.Q.D.' Phillips replied.

The humour of the situation appealed to me. I cut in with a little remark that made us all laugh, including the captain. 'Send S.O.S.,' I said; 'it's the new call. It may be your last chance.' Phillips, with a laugh, changed the signal to 'S.O.S.'

D One survivor said . . .

I only realized the situation was serious when I saw a working-class passenger on the first-class deck.

E . . . and another said in 1982:

We were going far too quickly through the ice. And if only there'd been enough lifeboats, no one need have died.

1 Copy out and complete this paragraph:

The *Titanic* set out on her maiden voyage from _____ in April _____. The *Titanic* was the _____ ship of the time and her owners said that she was 'practically _____'. However, she hit an _____ in the Atlantic _____ and more than _____ people died.

2 Are the pictures on page 12 primary sources? Give reasons for your answer.

3 a) How many lifeboats was the ship originally designed to have?

b) How many people would these have carried? (They were the same size as the final ones.)

c) How many people did the lifeboats on the finished ship carry?

d) Why were the first lifeboats not full?

e) Why could the disaster have been worse?

4 How can you tell that some of the passengers *and* crew did believe she was 'unsinkable'?

5 a) Which class of passenger suffered worst?

b) What does the evidence tell you about class attitudes at that time?

c) Look at the drawing on page 12. Why did the first and second classes have more survivors?

6 Discuss who you think was most to blame for the loss of the *Titanic*.

4 The Suffragettes

hunger-strike white feather obese militant
suffrage Suffragette

In Edwardian Britain, there was a large gap separating the rich from the poor. But there was another which separated women from men. Men ruled the nation from Parliament – and women were expected to take a back seat. By 1900, some women no longer accepted this.

One of them was a widow, Mrs Emmeline Pankhurst. In 1903, she started the Women's Social and Political Union (WSPU), along with her daughter, Christabel.

What they wanted was women's suffrage – in other words, votes for women. The *Daily Mail* called them 'Suffragettes'. They began by using the same peaceful methods which had been used in the 19th century.

When this had no effect, they decided to get public attention and support by being a nuisance. They shouted out at political meetings; they smashed shop windows; and some chained themselves to the railings outside Buckingham Palace.

What happened to a WSPU heckler in 1912.

Force-feeding a Suffragette – from a postcard of the time.

Many wound up in prison. They were pleased! Photographs were taken of them in prison uniform and they gave added publicity. The imprisonment gave them another weapon, too.

In 1909, one Suffragette in prison decided to go on **hunger-strike**. At first, the government just released hunger-strikers; later, they were force-fed through a tube in their nose and mouth.

Some MPs did support the idea of votes for women. In 1910 and 1912, there were attempts in Parliament to give votes to women but too many MPs still opposed the idea.

By then, anyway, the Suffragettes were losing sympathy and supporters. In 1913 and 1914, their campaign grew more violent. Houses and churches were burned down; bombs were let off; telegraph wires were cut; and acid was used to destroy putting-greens. Most famous of all, Emily Davison died after moving on to the race-track during the 1913 Derby race.

Many people thought this was more than being a nuisance; they regarded it as guerrilla warfare. So the government hit back. Its 'Cat and Mouse Act' of 1913 let it release hunger-strikers so they could get better. As soon as they were healthy again, they were arrested and put back in prison.

But war clouds were gathering in Europe. When they finally broke in August 1914, Mrs Pankhurst told members to stop all action. Instead, its members began giving **white feathers** to men in civilian clothes. Although they had not won the vote, they were determined to help win the war.

This is "THE HOUSE" that man built,
And this is the Flag of the Woman's Franchise,
Which is making our Ministers open their eyes:
Fighting with grit, to the front bit by bit,
Determined in Parliament one day to sit,
The bold Suffragette who is sure to get yet
Into "THE HOUSE" that man built.

A and **B** Two postcards, giving different views of the Suffragette campaign.

THIS IS "THE HOUSE" THAT MAN BUILT

THE HOUSE that our Statesmen for years have controlled Ruling the world with mind fearless and bold; Can Woman expect To rule such a HOUSE She that's afraid of a poor little mouse: NO! NO!! Suffragette your place is not yet, Inside THE HOUSE that man built.

C The *Daily Sketch* described one demonstration in 1910:

120 ARRESTED

Suffragist Attack on House of Commons

DISGRACEFUL SCENES

Reckless Women Charge Headlong Into Cordon of Police

True to their word, the Suffragists marched on the House of Commons yesterday and the scenes exceeded in violence the excesses of which these **militant** women had previously been guilty.

It was a picture of shameful recklessness. Never before have otherwise sensible women gone so far in forgetting their womanhood.

Here, [one] campaigner sprawled in the mud, to the obvious disgust of decent men, and the obvious delight of some others. There, an **obese** champion of the vote flung her bedraggled self against smiling policemen until lack of breath beat her. A few of the more desperate pushed at the police in Rugby style until they were swung back by a powerful neck or waist grip.

Arrests were only made in extreme cases, and many women were sadly disappointed at not being 'run in'. Even so, 120 people were taken into custody, including a number of men.

The first deputation of women was led by Mrs Pankhurst. They came from the Council of War at Caxton Hall, where a frantic assembly of excited women had listened to the [advice] of their leaders.

The 'deputation' was, of course, informed that Mr Asquith could not see them. An almost immediate tussle ensued with the police. The police snatched the banners and flung them into the moat and a strong barrier of police was formed in front of the entrance to St Stephen's. By this time, relays had arrived, and the suffragists numbered about 300. Reckless attempts were made to break the strong front of the police.

1 Explain the meaning of these words: suffrage; Suffragette; hunger-strike; force-feeding; 'Cat and Mouse Act'.

2 a) Which of the pictures on page 14 is a primary source? Give reasons for your choice.
b) Which pictures are propaganda?

3 a) Look at the photograph on page 14. What do you notice about the crowd?
b) What do you think is happening?

4 a) Look at evidence A and B. Which one supports the Suffragettes?
b) In what way is the *other* one biased?
c) Which one do you think shows the woman as most feminine? Why did it do this?

5 a) Read evidence C. Is this biased for or against the Suffragettes? Quote any words which show this.
b) Rewrite this news item in an unbiased way, using the facts in the article.

6 a) Mrs Pankhurst argued that 'The argument of the broken window pane is the most valuable in modern politics'. Explain what she meant.
b) What are the dangers of these tactics?
c) What else could the Suffragettes have done to get publicity?

5　The First World War

Oh! We don't want to lose you
But we think you ought to go,
For your King and your Country,
Both need you so.

HOW THE SIDES LINED UP FOR THE GREAT WAR

TRIPLE ALLIANCE
Germany
Austria-Hungary
Italy

Versus

TRIPLE ENTENTE
France
Russia
Great Britain

alliance Dreadnought mobilised ultimatum
prophecies assassinated
infantry sniper 'Trench foot' armistice
conscription munitions zeppelin rationing
Schlieffen Plan Triple Alliance
Triple Entente No man's land

War clouds had been gathering for some time, despite the fact that European politicians had been busy trying to avoid war. Ever since 1879, major European countries had been making **alliances** and agreements to keep the peace.

By 1914, all the major European powers were caught up in this web of agreements. But, instead of making the countries feel safer, it only increased their fears. If one country went to war, there was a risk that others would get dragged in. And that is what happened.

At the heart of the web was Germany, which had not existed as a separate country until 1871. Now, she was large and powerful. On either side of her, France and Russia saw this as a threat.

When the Germans began to build up their navy, Britain, too, began to distrust Germany. The Germans built more ships; so did Britain. Then,

the British developed a more powerful battleship, the **Dreadnought**; so did Germany. Meanwhile, all the main countries, except Britain, were training huge reserve armies which could be quickly used in an emergency.

The Germans, too, were worried. They feared an attack by France and Russia at the same time. So the German Chief of Staff, von Schlieffen, had drawn up a plan. The idea was to defeat France quickly and then switch to face Russia.

But there was a problem. The Germans planned to pass through Belgium to attack France. However, back in 1839, Britain had promised to help Belgium if she was attacked. But in the summer of 1914, this seemed unlikely.

Then, on June 28th, Archduke Franz Ferdinand was shot dead by a Serbian student called Gavrilo Princip. For a few days, the event was in the news, before most people forgot about it. Apart from anything else, there was tennis at Wimbledon to think about.

But the Archduke had been heir to the throne of Austria – and Austria did not forget about it. Austria sent Serbia an **ultimatum**: let our officials into Serbia or we declare war. Serbia said No. On July 28th, Austria declared war.

Germany supported Austria. On August 2nd, Germany asked Belgium to allow German troops to march through the country to attack France. Belgium said No. Germany marched in anyway and, that same day, Britain declared war on Germany. The First World War had begun.

At first, it was probably the most popular war ever. All over Europe, men rushed to join up. People waved and laughed as the troops set off. After all, everybody said, it would be over by Christmas. But they were wrong.

Experts had given reasons why there'd be no war.

1 Write one sentence about the part each of these people played before the war:
von Schlieffen; Archduke Franz Ferdinand; Gavrilo Princip; Sir Edward Grey.

2 a) Draw the map on page 16.
b) In different colours, shade in the countries in the Triple Alliance and the Triple Entente.
c) Why do you think (i) Britain had a bigger navy than other countries but (ii) a smaller army?

3 a) Read the written evidence. For *each* piece of evidence, write down words which describe the writer's feelings. These words may be useful: surprised; delighted; sad; enthusiastic; hopeful; fearful; brave.
b) Explain why most people were first surprised, then pleased.
c) Why do you think most people did not agree with Lord Kitchener?

4 If there were a war tomorrow, would your feelings be the same? Give reasons.

A Harold Macmillan, a university student in 1914, wrote in 1966:

The First World War burst like a bombshell upon ordinary people. Had we been told in the summer of 1914 that in a few weeks all our little band of friends would rush to take up arms, that only a few [would] survive a four years' conflict, we should have thought such **prophecies** the ravings of a maniac.

B Sir Edward Grey was British Foreign Secretary in 1914:

The lamps are going out all over Europe; we shall not see them lit again in our lifetime.

C Agatha Christie, the crime writer, wrote in her autobiography

When an archduke was **assassinated** in far off Serbia, it seemed such a faraway incident – nothing that concerned us. After all, in the Balkans people were always being assassinated. That it should touch us here in England seemed quite incredible.

Swiftly, after that assassination, what seemed like incredible storm clouds appeared on the horizon. Extraordinary rumours got about, rumours of that fantastic thing – *War*! But of course that was only the newspapers. No civilised nations went to war. There hadn't been any war for years; there probably never would be again.

And then suddenly one morning *it had happened.* England was at war.

I received a wire from Archie [her fiancé]: 'Come Salisbury if you can hope to see me.' The Flying Corps would be among the first to be **mobilised**.

We had little time together. We had half an hour, no more. Then he said goodbye and left.

He was sure, as indeed all the Flying Corps was, that he would be killed, and that he would never see me again. He was calm and cheerful, as always, but all those early Flying Corps boys were of the opinion that a war would be the end, and quickly, of at least the first wave of them.

To me also it came with the same certainty that I was saying goodbye to him, I should never see him again. I remember going to bed that night and crying and crying until I thought I would never stop.

D Lord Kitchener was War Minister:

A nation like Germany, after having forced the issue, will only give in after it is beaten to the ground. That will take a very long time. No one living knows how long.

Fighting in the War

The war lasted over four years. There had been longer wars in history but the First World War was different: it was the first war to affect everyone. For long afterwards, people called it 'The Great War'. It was simply so awful that they did not want another one.

It was mainly an **infantry** war. French and British troops tried to stop the Germans from advancing to the Channel coast. Each side dug trenches. It was the same in the east, where Russians faced the Germans.

For four years, first one side and then the other tried to capture enemy trenches. Each side tried to hold on to them. In between them was a muddy wasteland, some 50 to 200 metres wide, called 'No man's land'.

To attack meant soldiers 'going over the top': they left their trenches and ran towards the enemy. The enemy tried to mow them down with machine-gun fire. Some just drowned in the mud.

Even if the attack succeeded, it usually made little difference. In 1917, about 250 000 British soldiers were killed or wounded at the battle of Passchendaele. When it was over, the survivors had advanced no more than 11 km – into a new set of trenches.

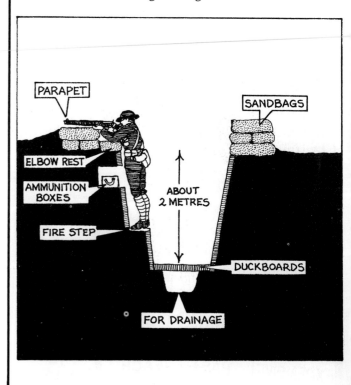

A What soldiers expected a trench to look like. This was how it was shown during training:

A soldier carried equipment which was about 1/3 of his own weight. For this, he was paid 5p a day.

In between attacks, men *lived* in these trenches. Rats swam in the water at the bottom; lice bred in the men's uniforms. Day after day, the trenches were shelled while the rifle-fire of **snipers** caught those who were careless. There was little time for sleep – or for changing clothes. Food was often late arriving, or cold.

'Trench foot' was a common problem from the start. The following spring, the Germans produced something worse: poisonous chlorine gas. After that, troops had to carry gas masks, as well as everything else. But they were little use against mustard gas, which came later. Meanwhile, the British introduced tanks in 1916.

German attacks on American ships helped bring the United States into the war in 1917, although Russia pulled out a few months later. But it was 1918 before a land attack at last succeeded and German troops were pushed back. An **armistice** was signed and fighting stopped at 11 a.m. on November (the eleventh month) 11th, 1918.

That afternoon, the British Prime Minister, Lloyd George, told the House of Commons, 'I hope we may say that this fateful morning came to an end all wars'. He was still alive in 1939 to discover that he was wrong.

B The real thing – an Australian trench:

C George Morgan was 18 when he fought at the Battle of the Somme in 1916. Sixty years later, he described it:

We formed into one line and walked slowly forward. We had only gone a few yards when my mate, Billy Booth, was hit. Then the man on my left fell against me. Lines of men were just disappearing. The Germans' machine guns fired at us like it was target practice.

The wire was 60 yards away but only a few made it as far as that. They became fastened on the barbs and the machine guns tore their bodies to shreds. It was all over in ten minutes.

It was an absolute fiasco. A slaughter. The best of our generation died there. That's why the country hasn't been the same since. The commanders didn't care about us. I don't think they bothered about human life.

D Over 1 million men from Britain and the Empire died. This was how one family learned of their son's death:

Dear Mr and Mrs Culling & Family.
It is my painful duty to inform you that your beloved son George succumbed to wounds received yesterday Monday March 20th.
I am sure it will come as a terrible shock to you all.
For indeed it has come likewise to us. He was indeed very popular with us all.
Although it will have cast a very dark cloud over you all, I think you can indeed see a silver lining. For he has died a most glorious death and has shown the country he was a true British soldier.
If you can see it in this light your loss is George's eternal gain.
Trusting that God will give you strength to bear your terrible strain
I Remain Your
In Sympathy
Sapper. T. White.

E Captain Grenfell described trench life. He died in 1915.

I *adore* war. It is like a big picnic. I have never been so well or so happy. Nobody grumbles at one for being dirty. I have only had my boots off once in the last 10 days, and only washed twice.

1 Explain the meaning of these words: infantry; 'No man's land'; trench foot; sniper; armistice; parapet.
2 a) Draw evidence A on page 18.
   b) Write down at least two ways in which evidence B differs from your drawing.
   c) Think of two reasons why real trenches differed from your drawing.
3 Look at the lower drawing on page 18. Why do you think a soldier carried (a) a tool for digging; (b) sandbags?
4 a) Read evidence D. Write down three ways in which the writer comforts the family.
   b) Imagine you have just received a letter like this. Write a paragraph to describe your feelings.
5 a) Read the other evidence. Imagine you were a war reporter. What questions would you have asked a soldier in the trenches?
   b) Write down the answers he might have given you.

The Home Front

The Great War was the first war to affect everyone, even those staying at home. When it began, the government relied on volunteers for its army but more men were soon needed.

In 1916, **conscription** began. Bachelors went first; married men were called up later. By the end, about 6 million men had gone to fight and about 1 in 10 died.

It meant fewer workers at home, just when there was more work to do. So women took over the men's jobs, especially after 1916. No one would have dreamed of having women bus conductors before the war; now, they needed them. Women also found jobs on the railways, in shops and factories, and even as policewomen. In 1917, the Women's Land Army was formed to replace male farm labourers.

Meanwhile, other women were working in **munitions** factories. They had employed women before the war but, at last, people appreciated their work. Some of them worked an 80-hour week in dangerous conditions, handling powder which turned the skin yellow.

Only 1/3 of the conscripts were fit to fight.

The invention of aircraft and **zeppelins** meant that people suffered in another way, too. Britain was bombed for the first time. The east coast suffered most but, in 1917, 14 bombers made a daylight raid on London. There were nearly 600 casualties.

Meanwhile, German U-boats were attacking merchant ships bringing food across the Atlantic. Once, in 1917, only three weeks' food supply was left. Starvation was a real danger. In the following year, food **rationing** was started.

It was all necessary if Britain was to survive the war, let alone win it. Both rich and poor got used to their lives being very different compared with before the war. People even took their own sugar with them when they went visiting!

The government took control of far more than it had ever done before. It could even tell people where they had to work. The trade unions helped in the war effort and their membership went up.

Rich and poor people had been brought together by their life in the trenches. The war had helped to break down the barriers between the classes. But, when it ended in 1918, many rich people expected the old life just to start again. And the poor expected something better. Each group found it was wrong.

In 1915, the *Daily Mail* condemned short skirts which revealed the feet. But hemlines grew shorter, and so did hairstyles.

A A famous war poster:

Daddy, what did YOU do in the Great War?

B Zeppelin raids made headline news:

Air Raid Supplement

THURSDAY. MAY 13. 1915.

You English We Aare come + Well come again soon Kill or Cure

German

1. Zeppelin Airship (*Typical*).   2. Message the Germans Left Behind.
3. Unexploded Bomb in Westborough Road Schools Playground.

C Graham Greene recalled public reactions:

There were dramatic [events] even in Berkhamsted. A German master was denounced to my father as a spy because he had been seen under the railway bridge without a hat; a dachshund was stoned in the High Street; and once my uncle Eppy was summoned at night to the police station and asked to lend his motor car to help block the Great North Road. A German armoured car was said to be advancing [down it] towards London.

D Spy scares were common. An Essex vicar described one in his diary in 1916:

Here is a typical story of a German spy, told confusedly by a [local] woman.

'Well, you see, there was this cook in Braintree and she went out dressed like a cook but dined at the White Hart Hotel. She was dressed like a woman but had very large feet. She was probably a man dressed as a woman. Then she disappeared but, before she went, she prophesied that, after she had gone, zeppelins would come to Braintree and also go to Scotland. And it all turned out as she said. She was certainly a spy. Anyone with such big feet must have been a spy.'

1 Match up the dates on the left with the correct event on the right:

   1916   daylight German raid on London
   1917   the First World War ended
   1917   conscription began
   1918   Women's Land Army formed

2 a) Look at evidence A. Why do you think this poster was produced?
  b) What is the boy doing? Why should this affect the man?

3 a) Look at evidence B. Write down what you think the writing says.
  b) Why do you think they dropped the note?

  c) What effect would it have had on you?

4 a) Write down at least two major changes in women's fashion during the war.
  b) Why do you think these changes happened?
  c) Some people were shocked. Why?

5 a) Describe how people reacted in
  (i) evidence C and (ii) evidence D.
  b) Why did they react like that?
  c) Is there anything you do not believe about evidence D? Explain your answer.

6 Design your own recruiting poster. It should encourage unmarried men to join up in the days before conscription began.

6 The Twenties

Lloyd George had promised the troops that they would build a country 'fit for heroes' after the war. Briefly, all seemed hopeful. Trade did well in 1919 and 1920. It looked as though things were returning to normal.

It was only temporary. In 1921, unemployment shot up to over 2 million. Instead of building homes for heroes, 20 per cent of British builders were out of work. Spending cuts soon followed.

Savings included wage cuts and fewer houses.

Even ex-soldiers had their war pensions cut to save money. On Armistice Day, 1922, many unemployed ex-soldiers marched through London. Their banner said: 'From the living victims to our dead comrades who died in vain'.

But some people were still well-off and they wanted to forget about the war by having fun. In America, they called it 'the Roaring Twenties'. For the first time, Britain began to copy American entertainments. Hollywood films and **jazz** music were all the rage.

Going to the cinema had caught on during the war; by 1919, about half the population was going twice a week. Until 1927, there were only silent films, with a pianist adding an accompaniment. But the actors were stars, despite that. Charlie Chaplin, Rudolf Valentino and Mary Pickford were household names. So was Rin-Tin-Tin, 'the Wonder Dog'.

jazz   chaperone   flapper   Emancipation cocktail
Charleston

Above all, young people wanted to dance. Clubs which had dance floors were packed, especially if they had a jazz band. Along with the music came a whole range of new dances. The 'black bottom' was one of them; the 'Charleston' was the most famous.

The biggest change of all was in the lives of women. Many had worked for the first time during the war and enjoyed their new independence. In 1918, most women over 30 were given the vote; in 1928, it was given to all women over 21. Along with this equality came greater freedom.

The system of **chaperones** was dying out and unmarried women went to dance-halls on their own. Their new freedom showed in the way they dressed: they had short hair and wore straight dresses so they looked boyish. For them, it was a different world from that of 1914.

Fashionable **flapper** of the 1920s. Even having a suntan was new.

A This cartoon appeared in 1927:

SHADE OF OLD MILITANT : "So this is what I fought for !" *April 29th*, 1927.

B Fashion expert James Laver wrote in 1969:

In 1925 the post-war style appeared and all the young men were delighted. The more elderly of both sexes strongly disapproved. The Archbishop of Naples even went so far as to suggest that the recent earthquake in Amalfi had been due to God's anger at the exposure of the female leg. Birmingham waitresses were forbidden by their employers to wear short skirts.

In America a bill was introduced in Utah providing fines and imprisonment for women on the street with 'skirts higher than three inches above the ankle'. It was all of no avail. Skirts continued to get shorter and shorter until in 1927 they were shorter than they had ever been in the history of civilised costume – until our own day.

C The authoress Ethel Mannin recalled the 1920s:

The **Emancipation** of Women took place immediately after World War 1 and was in full swing in the 1920s. I know; having been born in 1900, I was *there*. Women cut off their hair and demanded the right to live their own lives on the same terms as men, and they did; women of all classes and all degrees of intelligence.

Drugs were not much part of the scene, but we drank a lot. There were all those **cocktail** parties and a cocktail-shaker was as much part of every properly equipped home, as a fridge nowadays.

'Children of the Jazz Age' our critics called us, and the 'Dancing Generation' – and with some justification, for we danced like mad, at all hours and in all kinds of places.

We were shallow and trashy, I suppose, in a way that young people today . . . are not, but we did bring tremendous zest to the business of living. We *had* 'the gaiety'. We had *fun*. The good-times mania was justified by the fact that it was an era in which it was possible to hope. The war-to-end-war had been fought and won. I would say that it was a more hopeful era than that which succeeded it.

1 Explain the part played by each of these in the 1920s: unemployment; spending cuts; American entertainments.
2 What was meant by (a) a country fit for heroes and (b) the writing on the banner in 1922?
3 a) Draw the lower picture from page 22.
   b) Look at the picture on page 20. What were the main changes in fashion between 1913 and the 1920s?
4 a) Look at evidence A. What are the three signs that the 'ghost' was a suffragette?
   b) What would have shocked her about the girl?
   c) What do you notice about the girl's skirt?

What does it mean?
5 a) In evidence B, why were people shocked by short skirts?
   b) Why would people today not be shocked by these fashions?
6 a) Read evidence C. Was the writer well-off or not? Explain how you decided.
   b) What does she think were the main features of her life in the 1920s?
   c) This woman was writing many years after the 1920s. What other sorts of evidence could we use to find out about the 1920s?

7 Marie Stopes

Jean, Jeannie, full of hope,
Read a book by Marie Stopes,
But, to judge by her condition,
She must have read the wrong edition.

contraception   abortion   matron
malnutrition   fatal

Look at the figures opposite. For the first 40 years of the 20th century, the birth rate was going down. Even today, it is well below the figure for 1900.

The biggest drop came between the wars for a number of reasons. Nearly 10 per cent of men aged between 20 and 45 died in the First World War, leaving nearly 2 million more women than men. So there were just fewer men to marry.

A second reason was that **contraception** was becoming easier to obtain, and safer. The pioneer of birth control advice was a remarkable woman scientist called Marie Stopes.

It all started because of her own unhappy marriage and divorce. Out of this experience, in 1918, she produced a book called *Married Love*. It was soon a best-seller.

Most of it was simply about marriage, but she did include a chapter on birth control. And it was this which attracted all the interest. Letters just poured in.

So she wrote another book, called *Wise Parenthood*. Then, in 1921, she opened the country's first birth control clinic at Holloway in London.

There were loud and bitter protests about the clinic, especially from doctors and priests. Many Catholic churchmen thought that birth control was little better than **abortion**. Her reply was that there might be fewer babies, but they would be healthier.

In any case, many women clearly needed advice. Although abortion was illegal, it was easy to get hold of drugs which caused an abortion. In three months, Dr Stopes had over 20 000 requests for abortions at her new clinic. She turned them down and gave contraceptive advice instead.

Her work helped all women, rich and poor. It meant the poor could avoid the burden of a large family; and all women could, if they wished, limit their family and concentrate on careers. It was yet another way in which women could demand equality with men.

A The birth rate in the 20th century. (Number of births per 1000 of the population.)

1900 – 27	1950 – 15
1910 – 25	1960 – 16
1920 – 24	1970 – 16
1930 – 16	1980 – 13
1940 – 14	

B Dr Marie Stopes:

C Dr Stopes studied her first 10 000 cases. These figures show the percentage of infant deaths and miscarriages, according to how many times the mother had been pregnant. (The official death rate for infants under one year was 8.3 per cent in 1921.)

1st – 11.9%	10th – 30.5%
2nd – 11.9%	13th – 40.0%
3rd – 11.9%	17th – 50.0%
5th – 27.3%	

Some early objections to birth control.

D This mother wrote to Dr Stopes in 1922:

Dear Dr Stopes,
   Could you be kind enough to tell me the safest means of prevention as I have had 14 children, 9 living. We are very poor people. **Matron** and doctor told me I had a very weak heart. If I have any more it might prove **fatal**. It's wicked to bring children into the world to practically starve.
Your faithfully,
Mrs N.G.

E Dr Jane Hawthorne told a meeting, 1921:

One of the cases is that of a woman of 39, and she has had 17 children. She was married when she was 19, and during these 20 years she has never been in normal health. During that long period she has been either nursing a baby or expecting the arrival of another. She is now, at 39, a very old woman. She has buried nine children who died at an early age of wasting diseases and **malnutrition**. Her husband is a labouring man and earns £2.37½ per week.

F Dr Stopes told the same meeting:

The second person who came to my clinic when it first opened came on behalf of a girl of 20 who was pregnant for the sixth time. And every previous time she had an abortion performed by her own mother. We, of course, had no help for that girl. We cannot deal with such cases.

G An early birth control advert (1926):

Recommended by the Medical Profession
"Wife's Friend"
The Public know
RENDELLS
It is a line tested and proved in all parts of the world, and every sale means a satisfied customer. *Every Genuine Box bears Autograph Trade Mark.*
W. J. RENDELL   **LONDON**

H A Family Planning poster (1970):

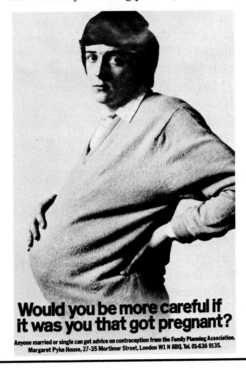

Would you be more careful if it was you that got pregnant?
Anyone married or single can get advice on contraception from the Family Planning Association. Margaret Pyke House, 27-35 Mortimer Street, London W1 N 8BQ. Tel. 01-636 9135.

1 Copy out and complete this paragraph:
   The pioneer of the birth control movement was _____ _____, who first wrote about it in her book called '_____ _____', which came out in _____. She received so many letters that she opened the country's first _____ in 1921 in _____, London.

2 Read all the evidence.
a) In evidence D, is the family rich or poor? Give reasons for your answer.
b) Why is she afraid of having more children?
c) How would contraception have helped the women in evidence D, E and F? Think of a different advantage for *each* case.
d) How would it have helped the rest of the family in D and E?

3 Look at the lower drawing on page 24. List the objections which people made. For each one, suggest how Dr Stopes could reply.

4 a) Write down the details in evidence C.
b) Give at least one reason why Dr Stopes' figures were different from the official ones.

5 a) Look at evidence G and H. What are the main differences between them?
b) Why is H so different?

8 The General Strike

1926

commission spats attrition
TUC

Sticker on a bus during the General Strike.

One industry in trouble after the war was coal-mining. Competition from abroad meant that profits were falling. In 1919, a **commission** recommended that the government should take over the mines from their private owners. It refused and, soon afterwards, miners' pay was cut.

In 1925, coal exports fell again. The mine-owners threatened another pay cut for miners – and longer working hours. The miners' leader, A J Cook, replied with the slogan, 'Not a penny off the pay, not a minute on the day'. Talks between the two sides got nowhere. On April 30th 1926, the mine-owners locked out the strikers.

This time, the miners had the support of the Trades Union Congress (TUC) and the TUC asked other workers to strike in sympathy with the miners. The government called it a General Strike but it mainly involved these unions:
* transport (buses, trams and trains)
* iron and steel workers * printers
* building workers * dock workers
However, the TUC had not really prepared any detailed plans for winning the dispute, whereas the government had. For months before, it had made

Trains were seen travelling backwards for miles trying to get on the right line.

A A London bus during the strike:

plans to distribute food and keep emergency services going.

It had other plans, too. From the second day of the strike, it began publishing its own daily newspaper, *The British Gazette*. It was also able to use the BBC to broadcast to the nation; union leaders and Labour MPs could not.

Above all, the government relied on volunteers to keep emergency services going. The middle classes mostly opposed the unions and thousands of them signed up as special constables for 25p a day. Meanwhile, businessmen, students and retired people helped by driving buses and trains or unloading ships.

The miners and many other workers wanted the strike to keep going but, after nine days, the TUC backed down. On May 12th, they called off the strike and people went back to work.

All except the miners. They were bitter because they felt that they had been deserted. Some held out for another six months until hunger and the winter forced them back to work – for longer hours and less pay. It was a defeat which the miners never forgot.

B The TUC thought their phones were tapped, so they used a code. This is part of it:

```
              IMPORTANT INSTRUCTIONS
                    C o d e

           I have found that a large number of telegrams
sent by despatch riders en route have never reached this
office.          It has therefore become necessary to
change our method of conveying information from the Despatch
Riders to the Transport Department.
     FROM WEDNESDAY, 12th MAY please DO NOT SEND TELEGRAMS,
but when important events or changes in the situation have
taken place, which were not known, as far as you are aware,
at the T.U.C. at the time of your departure, you are immedi-
ately to TELEPHONE VICTORIA 8016 Extension 8.
     There is no doubt that the telephonic messages are being
tapped.  It is essential, therefore, that the following code
should be used.  All that will be necessary will be to give
the name of the Driver, the Route Number, the Town and the
necessary code words.
     I shall be glad if you will kindly give this your close
attention.
                    C O D E

POLICE

Police...........................beauty
     baton charges.................beautify
Troops in control of ..........   beautiful.
     fired on crowds..............beautifully.

Property damaged by crowds a) shops or houses.....sweet
                         b) vehicles...........sweeter
                         c) railways or stations...sweetest

Persons injured by police or troops.(give number)....great
   "     killed  "    "    "     "    "     ".....greater.
ENGINEERS.................................echo
     serious increase of blacklegging
                    against engineers...........echoless
Engineers wavering..........................echoing
     returning to work.....................echoed.

RAILWAYMEN ................................Rain
   "   serious increase of blacklegging
                         against...........Rainless.
   "   Wavering............................raining
   "   returning to work ..................rained.
```

C One volunteer recalled:

I made my way to the engine sheds and was greeted by a man [dressed] in a silver grey suit, silver grey **spats**, silver velour hat, and lemon gloves. This vision said to me, 'I'm your fireman.' This shook me. The boiler was under pressure, and vibrating as boilers do under those circumstances. He turned to me and, pointing to the boiler, said, 'It's *boiling*.'

D From the *Daily Mirror*, May 7th:

THE EX-PREMIER'S DUTY.

The General Strike has been un-accompanied by any grave disorder. That is excellent. Everybody must keep their tempers under unrelaxing restraint. We deeply sympathise with the countless thousands of workers rendered idle by ukase of their so-called leaders. Mr. Thomas, Mr. Macdonald and Mr. Clynes know full well -- none better -- that the General Strike is a crime against the community. Let these three men be worthy of their citizenship and their leadership by obtaining the cancella-tion of the strike.   It is clearly Mr. Macdonald's duty as an ex-Premier to do this. He rightly holds the strike weapon in contempt. Why let the workers be fooled in the manner they are being fooled?

E Norman Pritchard was a miner who helped organise the strike in South Wales:

Conditions in the mines were very bad in those days of private ownership; I believe that many might find it difficult to believe the true facts.

With the ending of the General Strike it was generally understood that our fight would be one of **attrition**. A phrase we used was that the battle would be fought on the empty stomachs of our wives and children. The distress in the mining valleys was acute. My wife wrote to say that she had seen a number of young boys wearing potato sacks cut into trousers. I told my friends and they immediately began collections of old clothes and sent many loads direct to the Rhondda.

1 Write about the part played by each of these in the General Strike: A J Cook; the TUC; *The British Gazette*; volunteers.
2 In which *two* ways is the bus (evidence A) protected? In each case, explain why.
3 a) List the workers who went on strike.
   b) If you had been the TUC leader, which workers would you have chosen to strike, to ensure that it had a greater effect? Write down the groups you choose and give reasons why you picked them.
   c) The TUC called it a 'National Strike'. Do you think this is a better description than 'General Strike'? Give reasons.
4 How can you tell that the volunteer (in C) (a) is rich and (b) knows nothing about trains?
5 a) In evidence D, was the paper for or against the strike? Explain how you decided.
   b) What effect was this paragraph intended to have on the strikers?
6 a) Look at evidence B. What other words might the unions have needed to put in code?
   b) Write a brief telephone message in code to tell the TUC about the situation in your town during the strike.

Their father keeps their mother,
Their mother keeps their brother
And when they're running short of cash
They borrow from each other.

The number of unemployed dropped in 1927, the year after the General Strike. The future looked brighter in Europe, too. Six major countries, including Britain and Germany, signed the Kellogg Pact in 1928. It was an agreement *never* to go to war again. Over 50 other countries later signed it.

In the General Election of 1929, all the parties made an issue of solving the unemployment problem. The Labour Party won – but events in America were soon to end all hopes of finding a quick solution.

America had grown rich after the war; her industry had done well and people had money to spare. Some went on new luxuries, such as motor cars. But many people invested much of their new wealth in industry. They bought shares in companies which they hoped would make a profit. The value of these shares went up and up.

October 1929 brought a sudden **slump**. People began to lose confidence in these shares and started selling them. The more they sold, the more prices dropped. Firms went out of business; millions of people lost their jobs; even 5000 banks went **bankrupt**. Overnight, many rich people suddenly found they were broke.

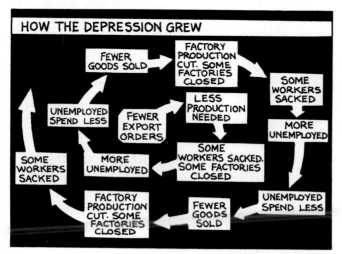

Countries such as Britain which exported goods to America soon felt the effects. *British* factories had to close down and *British* people lost their jobs. By 1930, unemployment had shot up to over 2½ million. By 1933, it had topped 3 million.

slump   bankrupt   pawnbroker   depression   petition
Means Test   Jarrow Crusade

How the Means Test worked.

Whole families suffered. Goods were regularly taken to the **pawnbroker**; some children stayed away from school because they could not afford to buy shoes; and the number of women dying in childbirth rose steadily.

The government, too, was in trouble. It was getting less money from taxes because so many people did not have a job. It was also paying out more in unemployment pay. Its first idea was to try to save money. It cut the wages of government workers. And it cut unemployment pay.

It did this by introducing a Means Test to check whether people had any other money coming in. If they had savings, they got less unemployment pay. If they had a grandfather living with them, his 50p pension was counted as income – and their money was cut. Some families turned out their old relatives just to avoid a cut.

A Unemployment in Great Britain (including Northern Ireland):

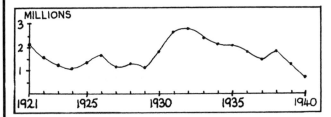

B This man had been a skilled engineer. He had been married about 20 years and had one son when he lost his job (1934).

Two years of unemployment found us in a bad way. At this period my wife had to enter hospital. Tradesmen were sympathetic and gave us credit, so a number of debts were contracted. After her recovery she returned to work. Life became more and more strained. There were constant bickerings over money matters.

The final blow came when the Means Test was put into operation. I realised that if I told the Exchange that my wife was earning a little they might reduce my benefit [so] when I was sent a form on which to give details of our total income I neglected to fill it up. For this, I was suspended benefit for six weeks. This was the last straw.

Eventually, after the most heartbreaking period of my life, both my wife and son, who had just commenced to earn a few shillings, told me to get out, as I was living on them and taking the food they needed.

I left and took with me a little furniture. I rented an unfurnished bedroom for 22½p a week. This happened some fifteen months ago. Since then, I have drawn 76p weekly from the dole and have had to sell every bit of furniture. I have never been able to afford coal for a fire. The outlook as far as I am concerned is hopeless. I've given up dreaming of any return to my former life and work, and just hang on hoping something big will happen before I die.

C A Birmingham health visitor described one family she visited:

Mrs J.'s husband has been out of work 14 weeks and there's five of them starving on 75p a week. Mrs J., a young woman of 26 had, as the neighbours said, 'gone away almost to a skeleton' through sheer starvation. Though she was nursing her baby, I found that all the food she herself had had yesterday was a cup of tea at breakfast-time, and tea and two slices of bread and butter, provided by a married sister living near, at tea-time.

From the husband's unemployment pay of £1.00 a week, 25p had to go to pay off a debt, 31p for rent, and only 44p was left for food and fire. A school dinner for the eldest child was divided with his four-year-old brother every day and saved them from utter starvation.

D One man walking in Whitehall in the 1930s:

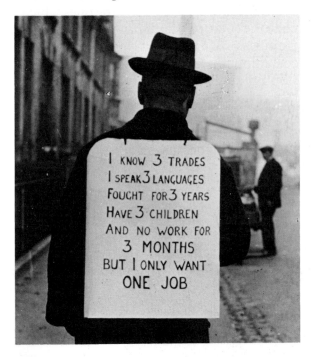

1 a) Draw the graph in evidence A.
   b) In which year was unemployment worst?
   c) Is this better or worse than nowadays?
2 a) What was the reason for the Means Test?
   b) Explain how the Means Test worked.
   c) Do you think it was a good system or not? Give reasons for your answer.
3 a) Look at evidence D. Why was this man walking round with a board on his back?
   b) Which of the things written on the board would make him most bitter? Give reasons.
4 a) Read evidence B. What were the results of the Means Test for this family?
   b) Which of these words describe the man's feelings: hopeless; depressed; unlucky; hopeful; poor; lazy; comfortable; bitter? Give reasons for those you choose.
5 a) Read evidence C. What are the signs that this family is poor?
   b) Think carefully. Why is Mrs J eating so little? What *two* results may this have?

North and South

There was another side to life in the 1930s. For those who had a job, wages were probably going up. Workers were 50 per cent better off in 1938 than they had been in 1924. Food was cheaper; so were the new motor cars and radios. People could go and watch one of the new talking pictures for just 2½p.

Some industries were doing well, too, and a number of new ones had started up, creating new jobs. Plastics, artificial fabrics and the electric industry were all new and thriving.

But many of the new factories were built in southern England so job prospects were much better there than in the north. Many people in the south had no idea of how deeply the **depression** was affecting the other half of Britain.

This was because the industries which suffered most were Britain's oldest ones – the ones which had made the country wealthy during the 18th and 19th centuries. The worst-hit were:

* coal mining   * iron and steel
* shipbuilding   * textiles (wool and cotton)

All these industries were based on, or near, coalfields. And, in the mining towns, nearly everyone was affected by the depression. Many shops closed down because families on the dole bought less.

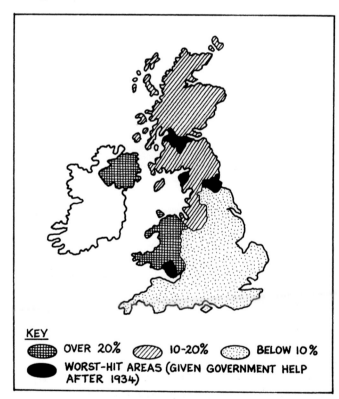

KEY
- OVER 20%
- 10-20%
- BELOW 10%
- WORST-HIT AREAS (GIVEN GOVERNMENT HELP AFTER 1934)

The figures show the percentage of workers unemployed in 1937. In the south-east, the figure was only 6 per cent.

FOOD EACH WEEK

MEAT 655g	FLOUR 1.8 kg	MILK (FRESH & CONDENSED) 1 LITRE
EGGS 1½	BUTTER & MARGARINE 212g	CHEESE 51g
POTATOES 1.5 kg	FISH 76.5g	FRUIT & VEGETABLES 850g

WHAT THE SMITH FAMILY ATE

| BREAKFAST | DINNER | AFTERNOON | NIGHT |
| Tea, bread and margarine | Stew or boiled fish, potatoes, bread, tea | tea | Cocoa, bread and margarine |

The drawings show how much food it was estimated that people earning up to 50p a week could afford in 1934. The Smith family (see the evidence) had an income of £2.37½ a week. Their typical food on a weekday is shown here.

The Jarrow Crusade

One of the worst-hit places was the shipbuilding town of Jarrow, on the River Tyne. The shipyards had been making Jarrow prosperous even as recently as the Great War; in the 1930s, their decline brought poverty.

World trade had slumped. There were fewer orders for ships. In fact, there was not one new order for a ship from Jarrow in 1932. In 1934, the yard closed down. About 75 per cent of the male workers had no job.

In 1936, they decided to try to attract publicity. Their local MP, Ellen Wilkinson, led a march of 200 unemployed men to London. It was a peaceful demonstration which was received warmly along the 480-kilometre route.

It was a different matter at the House of Commons, when they handed in a **petition**. One member of the government said he had heard that things were getting better in Jarrow. The Prime Minister gave them tea – but no promises.

And that was all. They went home by train to find their dole had been cut because they had not been 'available for work'.

A Alfred Smith was unemployed in 1939. This picture was printed by *Picture Post* and shows the family eating their main meal – boiled fish, dry bread and tea:

B The same photograph – or is it?

C These extracts are from the same issue:

Alfred Smith lives at 52, Leo Street, Peckham. His face is lined, and his cheeks are sunken, because he has no teeth. He is only 35 years old.

When Alfred Smith married 12 years ago, he was a skilled workman, earning good wages. Things went well with him for nine years. But then the chemicals used in his work made his teeth rot, so that they had to be extracted. He fell ill, was away from work for five weeks, and lost his job. He has not had a regular job since.

Before he lost his job, Smith had ordered artificial teeth and paid 75p towards their cost. He has never been able to get them finished. That is why his cheeks are sunken.

They have had seven children. Three died. Frances, aged 9, suffers severely from rheumatism because her home is damp. Peter and John are ailing; and Smith gets 20p a week extra for them.

Like all other able-bodied unemployed, Smith covers big distances looking for work.

If he is not too far off by then, Smith goes home for his midday meal, then goes out again looking for work. [Afterwards] he goes home to help his wife – who has been ill, and is not strong – does some cleaning up, potters about, goes into the street to talk to his friends, plays with his children. And so his days pass, slowly.

Smith does not whine: but he feels he has some just complaints. He has lost the feeling of bewilderment and helplessness that came on him when he first lost his job, saw his savings melt away, became dependent on the dole and the kindness of officials.

He has kept his spirit through three long years of disappointment. But he is beginning to feel that perhaps there is no longer a place for him in our scheme of things, that he must change it or perish. He wants work, he cannot find it. And Alfred Smith is only one of two million.

---

1 Copy out and complete this paragraph:
  People in the _____ of England were less affected by the depression than people in the north. New industries, such as _____ and _____ provided new jobs, and people in jobs were 50 per cent better off in _____ than in _____.

2 a) Draw the map on page 30.
  b) Look at the areas of bad unemployment. How do these compare with job prospects today?

3 a) Why did the Jarrow march take place?
  b) Why do you think they chose that way of getting publicity?
  c) What other methods could they have used?

4 Look carefully at the evidence on this page.
  a) How is evidence A different from B?
  b) Why do you think the picture was changed?
  c) What feelings does the writer of C want the reader to have?
  d) Is evidence C unbiased or not? Give reasons for your answer.

5 a) Look at the top drawing on page 30. How does this compare with evidence E on page 9?
  b) How does it compare with *your* diet today?

10 Into the Motoring Age . . .

**assembly line
mass-producing
commute**
Belisha beacon

At one time, there were 96 car firms. These were some of their symbols.

In 1900, there were still far more horses than cars on the roads of Britain, but the situation had changed completely by 1914. Between those years, motor taxis had replaced horse-drawn cabs and buses with petrol engines had taken over from the old horse buses. People with money had followed the lead of King Edward VII; motoring had become fashionable.

But it was still expensive. Cars were hand-built and few people could afford them. The man who changed that was a former cycle-repairer called William Morris. He visited America and saw the **assembly line** used by Henry Ford to make his cars.

Back in Britain, Morris began **mass-producing** cars after 1919. So did Herbert Austin. Each believed there was a big demand for small, family cars, provided they were cheap.

Faced with the slump in 1921, Morris reacted by cutting his prices. Sales rocketed up and others copied. The Austin 7 of 1922 cost just £165. Indeed, car prices actually fell by 50 per cent between 1924 and 1936.

At last, days in the country or at the seaside were within the reach of many people. Days out by car became popular – the Austin 7 did a steady 64 kph! People were also choosing to live in villages and **commute** to work. But, the more cars there were, the more problems they caused.

In 1933 and 1934, there were over 7000 fatal accidents each year so the Ministry of Transport at last took action. Its safety campaign brought deaths down to around 6500 a year.

One group of motorists did not affect other road users or cause traffic jams or spoil the countryside. They were the racing motorists. Motor races became popular entertainment in the 1930s.

British cars were then amongst the best in the world. Britain held the land speed record throughout the 1930s. By 1939, the speed was up to 595 kph.

Motorbikes, too, were more common. Or, for those less well-off, a bicycle cost just £3. But it was the car which was doing most to change people's lives – and it has gone on doing so ever since.

ROAD SAFETY MEASURES
1908 ROAD SIGNS
1924 WHITE LINES ON ROADS
1926 TRAFFIC LIGHTS
1934 BELISHA BEACONS
30 SPEED LIMIT
DRIVING TESTS FOR NEW DRIVERS

A In 1932, *Every Boy's Hobby Annual* predicted that the 'car of the future' would look like this:

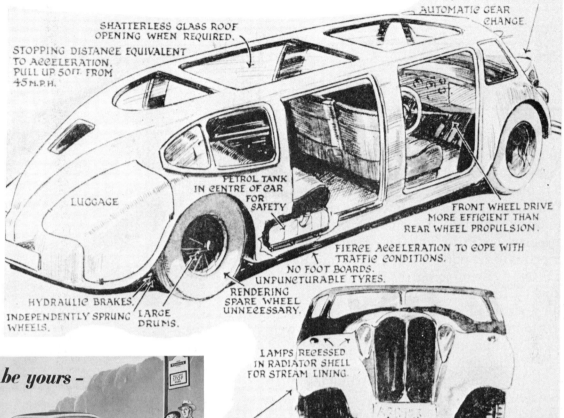

PERFECTED ENGINE 8 CYL. V TYPE NOT ACCESSIBLE ~ NOT REQUIRING ATTENTION.

AUTOMATIC GEAR CHANGE.

SHATTERLESS GLASS ROOF OPENING WHEN REQUIRED.

STOPPING DISTANCE EQUIVALENT TO ACCELERATION, PULL UP 50 FT. FROM 45 M.P.H.

LUGGAGE

PETROL TANK IN CENTRE OF CAR FOR SAFETY

FRONT WHEEL DRIVE MORE EFFICIENT THAN REAR WHEEL PROPULSION.

FIERCE ACCELERATION TO COPE WITH TRAFFIC CONDITIONS.

NO FOOT BOARDS. UNPUNCTURABLE TYRES. RENDERING SPARE WHEEL UNNECESSARY.

HYDRAULIC BRAKES. INDEPENDENTLY SPRUNG WHEELS. LARGE DRUMS.

LAMPS RECESSED IN RADIATOR SHELL FOR STREAM LINING.

VERY LOW BODYWORK.

NEW THREE LETTER PLATE OLD TWO LETTER STYLE NOW RUNNING OUT.

It can be yours –

THE £100 FORD SALOON

B A car advertisement of 1935.

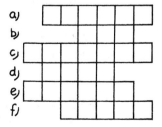

a) King who made motoring popular.
b) Probably petrol-driven by 1914.
c) Road crossing beacons named after him.
d) Drivers did not need one until 1934.
e) He mass-produced cars after the war.
f) White ones made roads safer!

1 Copy out this grid and fill in the spaces, using the clues in the right-hand column.

a)
b)
c)
d)
e)
f)

2 a) Look at the safety measures in the lower picture (page 32). For each one, explain why roads were dangerous without it.
  b) Which one do you think was most important?
3 Look at evidence B. What sort of customer was this car aimed at? (There are two clues in the advert. Write down those you spot.)
4 a) Look at evidence A. Which of these changes has happened since 1932?
  b) Draw or write about what you think a car of the 21st century will look like.
5 Look at the car symbols on page 32. Which of these firms are still making cars today?

11 . . . and the Flying Age

supersonic

Apart from a few airships, the history of powered flight belongs entirely to the 20th century. In 1903, two Americans called Wilbur and Orville Wright made a plane which stayed in the air for 59 seconds.

At first, few people were interested. But, soon, there was no shortage of people trying to prove what a plane could do. The *Daily Mail* was quick to offer prizes to get publicity. In 1909, Louis Blériot won £1000 by flying across the English Channel. It took just 37 minutes.

But it was the First World War which boosted efforts to improve aeroplanes. By 1918, they were flying at 240 kph, twice the average speed of 1914. They were also flying higher.

In 1919, John Alcock and Arthur Whitten-Brown flew non-stop across the Atlantic Ocean; in 1927, Charles Lindbergh flew solo from New York to London in under 34 hours.

The Second World War also encouraged development. A British scientist, Sir Frank Whittle, had invented the jet engine and the first British jet aircraft, the *Gloster*, flew in 1941. Jet passenger planes became common in the 1950s.

In fact, it was the rapid growth of passenger travel which most affected people in general. In 1919, a service from London to Paris could carry two or three passengers for £20 each. By 1932, Britain's Imperial Airways was taking up to 20 passengers to Australia. It took just twelve days, instead of at least 4 weeks by sea. By 1939, air routes linked most major cities in the world.

Today, air travel makes it possible for millions of people every year to go on holiday to places which, in 1900, could only have been reached by the rich. Many are carried in huge planes, such as jumbo jets, which can carry 500 passengers.

Meanwhile, businessmen can use the **supersonic** airliner *Concorde*. It was built by the British and French, working together, at a cost of over £900 million. No one expects that it will ever make enough profit to cover its initial costs.

A An Imperial Airways poster:

EVERY IMPERIAL AIRWAYS AIR LINER HAS

4 ENGINES FOR SECURITY

IMPERIAL AIRWAYS
in 1937 carried over 70,000 passengers and flew over 6,000,000 miles

1 Here are the names of four key people in the history of flight. Unscramble the letters to find out who they are and write about the part each of them played.
a) WINK A F HITLER; b) J C COOL HANK;
c) WILUW BRIGHT; d) BILL REOTIOUS.

2 a) Look at the advertisement above. What is it stressing – and why?
b) In what two ways does it do this?
c) Why do modern airlines advertise their comfort rather than their safety?

3 a) Read page 35. Describe Amy Johnson's career in your own words.
b) If she were alive today, which parts of her story would almost certainly be different? Give reasons for your answer.

AMY JOHNSON ~ FAMOUS FEMALE AVIATOR

AMY JOHNSON CAME FROM HULL.

SHE FIRST FLEW WHEN SHE WAS 17: "I WAS CRAZY ON FLYING."

SHE GOT A JOB IN A SOLICITOR'S OFFICE, AND STARTED FLYING LESSONS IN LONDON...

...THEY COST HER £2·00 AN HOUR.

SHE BECAME THE FIRST WOMAN TO GET A GROUND ENGINEER'S LICENCE.

HER PARENTS BOUGHT HER A SECONDHAND GYPSY MOTH...

...IT COST £600

1930

SHE HAD NEVER FLOWN OUTSIDE ENGLAND...

AUSTRALIA

...BUT SHE DECIDED TO FLY SOLO TO AUSTRALIA AT THE AGE OF 26.

"THE COCKPIT LOOKED LIKE A VILLAGE STORE"...

...AND SHE CARRIED A SPARE PROPELLER.

IT WAS AN EVENTFUL FLIGHT...

SHE HAD TO LAND IN THE PERSIAN DESERT IN A SANDSTORM...

...AND SHE CRASH-LANDED IN BURMA.

LUCKILY, IT WAS NEAR AN ENGINEERING COLLEGE. THEY REBUILT THE 'PLANE.

IN THE PACIFIC, SHE LANDED IN A JUNGLE

...BUT SHE WAS TAKEN TO A FRENCH MISSIONARY.

THE FLIGHT TOOK 20 DAYS.

WHEN SHE LANDED IN AUSTRALIA, SHE WAS TREATED AS A HEROINE.

IN THE WAR, SHE JOINED THE AIR TRANSPORT AUXILIARY. IN 1941 SHE CRASHED IN THE THAMES ESTUARY. THEY FOUND WRECKAGE BUT HER BODY DID NOT TURN UP. SOME PEOPLE BELIEVE SHE WAS ON A SECRET MISSION. THE FULL FACTS HAVE NEVER BEEN MADE PUBLIC.

Her plane crashed in Thames Estuary . .

Amy Johnson bales out—is missing

Daily Express Air Reporter BASIL CARDEW

AMY JOHNSON, the world's first famous woman pilot, is missing, believed drowned. A military airplane she was flying crashed into the Thames Estuary on Sunday.

A patrol boat skimmed across the water when shore watchers reported having seen the pilot bale

12 Political Change

coalition   minority
Fascist   Communist

In 1900, over 100 people held a meeting in the City of London. They were a mixed bunch: some were from trade unions; others represented organisations such as the new Independent Labour Party. But all of them wanted the working classes to be represented in Parliament.

They decided to start a new organisation called the Labour Representation Committee. Its aim was to get Labour MPs elected to Parliament and start a new political party. This party would represent the workers and stand up for their interests.

The future did not look too hopeful. The new group had hardly any money; it did not even have total working-class support. The miners, for instance, had an agreement with the Liberal Party and at first stayed out of the group.

Yet, when a general election was held later that year, two Labour MPs were elected. One of them was Keir Hardie, who had started work as a messenger-boy, earning 12½p a week.

It was a very small beginning. At first, it made little difference to the two main political parties – the Liberals and the Conservatives. But support for the LRC grew. In the election of 1906, 29 MPs were elected and they now called themselves the Labour Party. The two-party system of British politics had been broken.

But the Labour Party's greatest help came from the Liberal leader, Lloyd George. In the First World War, Liberals and Conservatives had worked together. When it was over, he decided to carry on this **coalition** but many of the Liberal Party disagreed with him. The Party was split:

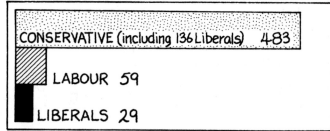

CONSERVATIVE (including 136 Liberals)   483
LABOUR   59
LIBERALS   29

Election results of 1918.

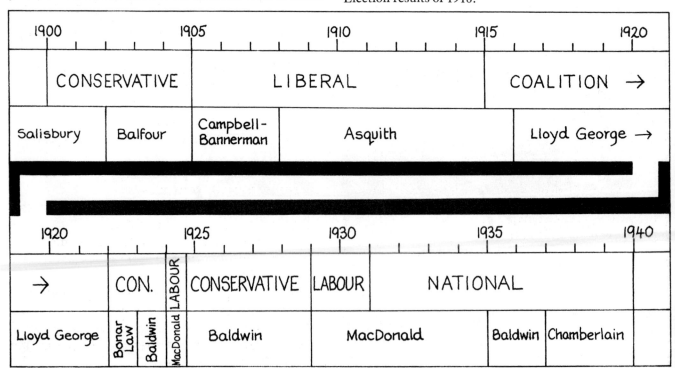

The Government and Prime Ministers of Britain from 1900 to 1940.

A Political poster for the 1931 election:

EQUALITY OF
SACRIFICE ?

THE MAN AT THE TOP:–
"Equality of Sac-rifice – that's the big idea, friends! **Let's all step down one rung!**"

J.F.HORRABIN

From 'PLEBS,' (Organ of the N.C.L.C.).

VOTE LABOUR

B This cartoon appeared in a trade union magazine in 1935:

Lloyd George: "Let me give you a 'New Deal' with these?"
Chorus from carriage: "No thanks. We're having a 'Square Deal' with these cards and on THIS TABLE"

The Liberal Party never recovered from this. For the first time, the Labour Party became the real rival of the Conservative Party. It was not just because the Liberal leaders had disagreed.

Workers were now better educated than ever before and wanted their own party. They no longer wanted to be governed by middle-class parties which they thought had different interests from their own.

This new party had problems in the years between the wars. It was briefly in power in 1924 and again in 1929 to 1931. Each time, it needed the support of the Liberals.

But the Liberal Party itself was losing support. Although it continued to get many votes, it never again formed a Liberal government. The Labour and Conservative Parties battled it out to run the country.

1 a) Which were the two main political parties in the 19th century?
   b) Which were the main parties by the 1930s?
   c) Which are the main parties today?
   d) Write down the names of any other parties about which you have heard.
2 a) Why did workers want their own party?
   b) What was their party first called?
3 a) Look carefully at evidence A. Which group of voters should it appeal to?
   b) How is it trying to warn the '£250 a-year' man?
   c) Which party do you think produced it? Give reasons for your answer.
4 a) Look at evidence B. What do the men in the train want? (Look at the table.)
   b) What is Lloyd George offering them?
   c) Why do you think the four men prefer what is on the table?
5 Are the two pieces of evidence propaganda or not? Give reasons for your answer.
6 Design your own poster for an election in the 1930s. Remember that unemployment was a key issue. Include a good slogan.

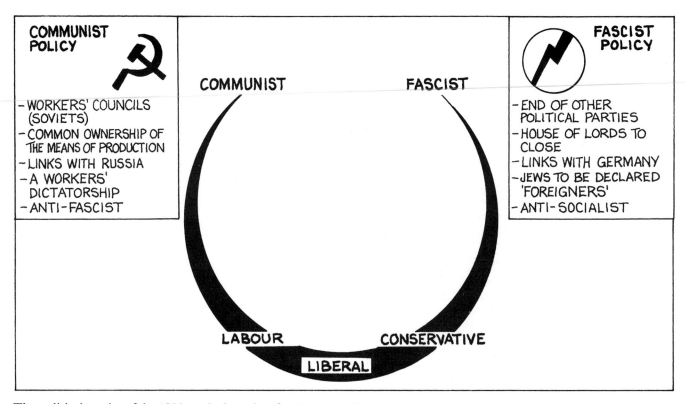

COMMUNIST POLICY

- WORKERS' COUNCILS (SOVIETS)
- COMMON OWNERSHIP OF THE MEANS OF PRODUCTION
- LINKS WITH RUSSIA
- A WORKERS' DICTATORSHIP
- ANTI-FASCIST

FASCIST POLICY

- END OF OTHER POLITICAL PARTIES
- HOUSE OF LORDS TO CLOSE
- LINKS WITH GERMANY
- JEWS TO BE DECLARED 'FOREIGNERS'
- ANTI-SOCIALIST

COMMUNIST   FASCIST

LABOUR   CONSERVATIVE

LIBERAL

The political parties of the 1930s and where they fitted on the political spectrum.

The three main political parties in the 1930s were Conservative, Labour and Liberal. But there were two other parties which had many thousands of supporters each. The diagram above shows them both.

The British Union of Fascists was founded in 1932 but no longer exists under that name; the Communist Party, which began in 1920, is still going today. These were **minority** parties; they put up candidates at elections but only one Communist MP was elected in the 1930s.

Even so, most people had heard of these parties and knew something about their ideas. After all, there had been a Communist revolution in Russia in 1917. Many Communist supporters thought there would eventually be a revolution in Britain, too.

Everyone knew about the Fascists. Mussolini, the Italian leader, was a Fascist; and Hitler, the German leader, had similar policies. And everyone had heard of them. British Fascists wore black shirts, like Mussolini's followers; they attacked Jewish shops, just as the German Nazis did. Some people thought that a Fascist party might come to power in Britain.

But the British voting system works against small parties. Neither party came to power. In the years afterwards, there has never been widespread support either for Fascist or Communist beliefs.

1 a) Draw the diagram at the top of this page.
b) Which two parties do you think would most disagree with each other?
c) What sort of people do you think supported the Communists? Give reasons.
d) Who do you think supported the Fascists? Again, give reasons for your choices.
e) Choose either the Communists or the Fascists and write what you think would have happened if they had won power in Britain.
2 Bring in to school a newspaper story about British politics today. Your group could make a collection of these.
a) For each news story, decide whether the writer is biased for or against one of the main parties.
b) What can you learn from these cuttings about the policies of the major parties?
3 After the revision exercises, the book goes on to cover the Second World War. Before you get to that section, ask your relatives if they have any objects connected with the war, such as ration books or a gas mask. They can be looking for them now and perhaps they would let you bring them in to school when you are studying the war.

Revision

1 This square includes the names of some of the people who have been mentioned in this book so far. They can read forwards or backwards, and across, down or sideways. Each time you find a name, write it down and write about who the person was and what he or she did.

```
S D A V S G E O R G E L
P A N K H U R S T I G E
O V D I N N W T O L R A
D I L O W Y G A R B O R
R D Z L S D S E D D E G
A S E B I T L E R X G M
W O I O T H O A K I D L
D N D O O O C P B O Y E
E E R T N W O R E S O T
R E A H N I L O U S L C
R Y H S Y S M I T H L M
Y E T O N I L P A H C K
```

2 There are always at least two ways of looking at any event. Here are eight headlines which could have appeared in newspapers between 1900 and 1930. They are about four events.
a) Pair up the headlines so that you have one biased for the event and one biased against it. Then, write down what the four events were.
b) For each event, write down a headline which is not biased.
c) Choose any one of them and write your own *unbiased* news story about it.

(1) GOD BLESS LLOYD GEORGE – FRIEND OF THE OLD

(2) GOVERNMENT UNDER ATTACK AS NATIONAL STRIKE HITS HARD

(3) THOUSANDS FACE MARVELLOUS FUTURE AS WONDERFUL CLINIC OPENS

(4) REVOLT AGAINST LAW AND ORDER AS GENERAL STRIKE BEGINS

(5) EVIL DOCTOR ADMITS: INNOCENT UNBORN BABES WILL DIE

(6) WRIGHTS' WEEDY ONE-MINUTE WONDER

(7) WICKED WELSH WIZARD'S GIVE-AWAY TO IDLE AGED

(8) OH, BROTHER! BRILLIANT BIPLANE SHOWS THE WAY

3 This advertisement of 1928 shows the range of electrical goods which were then on sale. All we have done is to remove the words telling you what these objects were.
a) Write down what you think they were.
b) Choose any two objects and describe how they differ from modern ones.

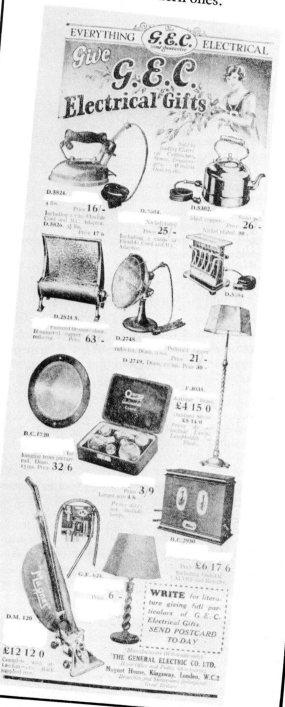

If you go down Munich way
Any fine September day,
You'll find them all
Doing the Hitler crawl.

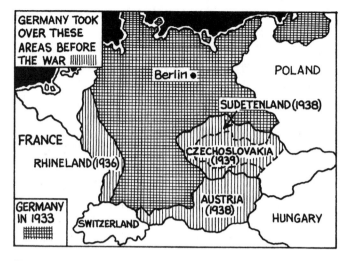

German expansion during the 1930s.

The unemployment situation grew brighter after 1936 but the situation in Europe grew gloomier. Hitler was re-arming Germany, and Italy had attacked Abyssinia. Both countries joined in the **civil war** in Spain. They were drawing closer together. It was a powerful and dangerous combination.

The British government was trying to avoid another major war. Its policy was called appeasement. It worked like this:

Many politicians felt that Germany had been unfairly treated in the Versailles Treaty at the end of the First World War. They argued that, if Hitler wanted to reject some details of the Treaty, that was understandable.

A A book of 1941 described public feelings about the Czechoslovakian crisis:

Nobody except the extreme Left felt quite sure why Britain should go to war, if at all. 'Who are them Sizzeks, anyway?' as country people asked. What right had 'Sizzeks' to rule over Germans (it was overlooked that the Sudetens had never formed part of Germany), and why should they not make concessions?

B The leaders meeting at Munich in 1938. From the left: Chamberlain, Daladier (the French PM), Hitler and Mussolini:

C From a government film of the time:

D Chamberlain described his feelings about the crisis:

How terrible, fantastic it is that we should be digging trenches and trying out gas masks here because of a quarrel in a far away country between people of whom we know nothing.

civil war   blackout
appeasement

They believed that Hitler would eventually be satisfied and war would be avoided. So Britain should show some 'give and take'. In the event, Britain gave – and Hitler kept taking.

Some people, such as Winston Churchill, warned against this policy. But few people paid much attention. Most people remembered the horrors of the First World War; they wanted to avoid another one at almost any price. This was the view of Neville Chamberlain, the British Prime Minister after 1937.

Although Chamberlain did not trust Hitler, he did think that Hitler did not really want to go to war any more than he did. So he agreed to Hitler's demand in 1938 to be given a part of Czechoslovakia, called the Sudetenland.

E A London bus conductor gave his views *before* the Munich meeting:

What the hell's he got the right to go over there and do a dirty trick like that? It'll have the whole world against us now. Who'll trust us? It's like throwing your own kid to the wolves. We helped make [Czechoslovakia] a country and then Chamberlain comes along and wants to buy that swine off. There'll be a war sooner or later, then there'll be nobody to help us.

F Chamberlain spoke on radio, September 3rd 1939:

You can imagine what a bitter blow it is to me that all my long struggle to win peace has failed. Yet I cannot believe that there is anything more or anything different that I could have done and that would have been more successful.

Up to the very last it would have been quite possible to have arranged a peaceful and honourable settlement between Germany and Poland, but Hitler would not have it.

His action shows that there is no chance of expecting that this man will ever give up his practice of using force to gain his will. He can only be stopped by force.

We and France are today going to the aid of Poland, who is bravely resisting this wicked and unprovoked attack on her people.

Chamberlain returned from talks with Hitler and waved an agreement they had signed. Each had promised never to go to war. Delighted crowds cheered at the news.

But opinion polls a few days later showed that most people thought Hitler was lying. When German troops marched into the rest of Czechoslovakia in March 1939, there was no longer room for doubt.

In fact, Chamberlain had good reasons for playing for time. First, Britain was not ready for a war. Second, everyone thought that this war would be even worse than that of 1914–1918. An official estimate reckoned that 600 000 people would die in the first six months of bombing over London. And who wanted that? (In fact only 61 000 died this way in the whole war.)

After March 1939, people prepared in earnest. More weapons were made; conscription was introduced for men of 20 and 21; sandbags went up round public buildings and trial **blackouts** were held.

When Germany invaded Poland on September 1st, 1939, it all became real. At 11.15 a.m. on September 3rd, Chamberlain spoke on BBC radio. Britain, he said quietly, was now at war.

---

1 Match up the dates on the left with the correct event from the right:

1919   Germany took the rest of
                    Czechoslovakia
October 1938   the Second World War began
March 1939   The Treaty of Versailles
September 1939   Germany took the Sudetenland

2 What were (a) appeasement; (b) blackouts; (c) conscription; (d) sandbags?

3 a) Draw the map on page 40.
   b) Shade in all the land which Germany controlled after March 1939.

4 a) According to evidence A, what was the people's attitude towards Czechoslovakia?
   b) How did the bus-driver in E disagree? Why was he against appeasement?

5 a) Why did Chamberlain want to avoid war?
   b) What does evidence C tell you about the kind of war people expected?
   c) How had Chamberlain's attitude changed by the time of his broadcast (evidence F)?

14 The Second World War

We'll meet again,
Don't know where, don't know when,
But I know we'll meet again
Some sunny day.

censored   Stuka   evacuated   Luftwaffe   Blitz
barrage balloon   Anderson shelter
air-raid warden
Dad's Army

The Second World War lasted six years, from 1939 to 1945. It began with people fearing a war even worse than the first one, and on a bigger scale. It ended with a new kind of warfare – the atomic bomb. In between, 50 million people died; 365 000 of them were British.

The Second World War is so recent that finding out about it ought to be easy. Nearly every month, there is a film or programme about it on television. Libraries have plenty of books about it. And many of you will have relatives who actually fought in it.

So this chapter is not about the fighting. It is about *how we know* about the fighting. We have put together a few items about the war. Some of your relatives can probably come up with items of their own, perhaps about members of your family. In this way, your group can build up its own evidence about the war.

Each piece of evidence needs to be studied carefully. Questions must be asked about it:
* Was the writer (or owner) actually there?
* When was it made or written?
* Was it produced for propaganda reasons?
* Is there any reason for it to be biased?
* What else can you find that will back up the evidence you already have?

A historian always needs to ask questions about his evidence. As you look at the evidence opposite, remember these problems:
* In a war, newspapers and radio are **censored**.
* Official papers are kept secret for years afterwards.
* A government must use propaganda to keep up the spirits of the people, especially if the war is going badly for them.

With those points in mind, look carefully at the evidence we have collected.

1 a) List the different kinds of evidence on page 43. For instance, A is a newspaper story.
b) Which one is not a primary source?
c) Give reasons why A and C may not have told the whole truth.
d) What sort of details might the writer of B have missed out, and why?
e) What feelings did Churchill try to create by his speech (D)? Choose from this list: anger; love; fear; hate; revenge; pride; sadness; determination. In each case, choose words from the speech to support your choice.
2 a) Which detail does evidence C repeat? Why?
b) What do you notice about the figures?
3 a) Which of these sources do you think tells you most about the war? Give reasons.
b) Is there any important kind of evidence which has not been used?
c) List as many other kinds of evidence as you can which an historian might use.

A From the *Daily Sketch*, December 19th 1939:

● . . . **A considerable proportion of the German cruiser strength has been sunk or put out of action in a single week . . . in the same week that the Graf Spee met her inglorious end ! . . . Mr. Churchill.**

Graf Spee Knew Battered Ships Awaited Her

MR. WINSTON CHURCHILL, First Lord of the Admiralty, revealed last night, in his broadcast speech, that the Graf Spee was scuttled outside Montevideo although only two damaged cruisers and one other cruiser, the Cumberland, awaited her.

The Captain of the Graf Spee knew, said Mr. Churchill, that the battleship Renown and the aircraft carrier Ark Royal were 1,000 miles away at Rio de Janeiro, taking in oil.

Graf Spee's 'Inglorious End'

In his description of the "Glorious Battle of the River Plate," he said of the defeated Nazi raider Graf Spee:

"Once in harbour she had the choice of submitting in the ordinary manner to internment, which would have been unfortunate for her, or of coming out to fight and going down in battle like the Rawalpindi, which would have been honourable to her.

"She discovered a third alternative. She came out, not to fight, but to sink herself in the fairway of a neutral state from whom she had received such shelter and succour as international law prescribes."

British losses in the battle, said the First Lord, had not been slight.

"There is no harm now," he added, "stating that the Ajax, in . . . was . . .

— **High Praise** — For Admirals

B A soldier wrote to his wife in 1942:

Darling girl,

At last your mail has begun to arrive. Thank you so much. I miss those kids badly. Could I have some good photos of you all soon?

The early morning and evening are the best times in the desert – wonderful sunrises and sunsets. In the evening, so peaceful except for gunfire if an attack is on or if the **Stukas** are diving, when the air trembles.

My great delight is the sea – the water is warm, warmer than I've ever felt it. You almost forget war until a life-jacket is washed in and you notice a little wooden cross on a raised mound nearby, bearing one word, 'Unknown'. Then comes the trudge back over the sands, past the ruins of a crashed bomber, the skeleton of what was once, maybe, a donkey and the ever-to-be-found rusty petrol tin. Then to the cookhouse for food. The tea is good, apart from a slight taste of petrol, but who can grumble?

Then we see an arrival of Gerry and Italian prisoners, dusty, torn and weary, alone with their thoughts of God-knows-what and we look at each other and think, 'Why the hell?' C'est la guerre.

C From a BBC news bulletin, September 15th 1940:

Here is the midnight news and this is Alvar Lidell reading it. Up to 10 o'clock, 175 German aircraft have been destroyed in today's raids over this country. Today was the most costly for the German air force for nearly a month.

In daylight raids, between 350 and 400 enemy aircraft were launched in two attacks against London and south-east England. About half of them were shot down. It was officially announced that, by ten o'clock tonight, 175 raiders were known to have been destroyed by our fighters and anti-aircraft gunners.

D Winston Churchill spoke on radio after the defeat of France:

The news from France is very bad and I grieve for the gallant French people who have fallen into this terrible misfortune. Nothing will alter our feelings towards them or our faith that the genius of France will rise again.

What has happened in France makes no difference to British faith and purpose. We have become the sole champions now in arms to defend the world cause. We shall do our best to be worthy of that high honour.

We shall defend our island and, with the British Empire around us, we shall fight on until the curse of Hitler is lifted from the brows of men. We are sure that, in the end, all will be well.

E A British film of 1964:

The Home Front

Everyone expected air attacks, so everyone had to get ready for them. As soon as war began, children were **evacuated** from the big cities to the safety of the countryside. One million of them left London to go to live with strangers. However, when no bombs fell, many of them went home again.

In July 1940, the **Luftwaffe** did begin to attack Britain, ready for a German invasion. **Barrage balloons** floated over southern England; searchlights lit up the night sky, looking for German bombers. In September, a **Blitz** of British towns began with night bombing raids on London.

When there was a raid, warning sirens went off. Everyone stopped what they were doing and took shelter. People rushed to take cover in their **Anderson shelters**; in London, thousands took their gas masks and went to sleep in the underground railway stations.

To make things difficult for the Germans, there was a blackout at night. **Air-raid wardens** patrolled streets, looking for any sign of light. Street lights stayed off and cars were driven with masked headlights.

How to Protect a Car
If you'll have to use a car on the roads, get a mattress ready now to fix on the roof. It and the roof will stop a bullet.

One magazine advised its readers to fix a mattress on a car roof – to stop bullets!

There were preparations in case Germans landed, too. Sign-posts were taken down; names were removed from railway stations. People were warned to look out for German spies.

Britain was organised as never before. The government could move people into essential jobs; some men were drafted into the coal-mines. Women were called up after 1941. Many of them joined the Women's Land Army to keep up food production.

WEEKLY RATIONS

Bacon or ham (113 gms) — Sugar (227 gms) — Cooking fat (227 gms) — Cheese (57 gms)

Tea (113 gms) — Meat ~6p worth (about 227 gms) — 1 pkt of dried eggs per month~ — ~and half an egg (about one a fortnight)

JAM — Tinned fruit — Baked beans — RATION Book

PEOPLE BOUGHT THESE ON A POINTS SYSTEM

Those men who were too old to fight joined the Local Defence Volunteers. People nicknamed them the 'Look, Duck and Vanish Brigade' or 'Dad's Army'. Eventually, they were armed but, at the start, there weren't enough rifles. Men even patrolled Blackpool Pier, armed with broomsticks!

There was not enough food, either. So, in 1940, the government introduced rationing and issued everyone with a ration book. Many items which were not rationed were soon hard to find. Razor blades, make-up and silk stockings were in short supply. Newly-weds sometimes had cardboard wedding cakes!

Meanwhile, the government encouraged people to grow more food themselves. Its slogan was 'Dig for Victory'. People dug up their roses and planted potatoes instead. Even school pupils were soon hard at work growing vegetables for school dinners.

CLOTHES WERE LATER RATIONED

OTHER GOODS WERE IN SHORT SUPPLY

Stockings were hard to find so girls used to plaster their legs with sand and water. When it dried, it was brushed off. The result? It looked as if they were wearing stockings!

44

A Children being evacuated in 1939:

B One man later recalled being evacuated:

We were given flannels and tooth brushes. We'd never cleaned our teeth up till then. And hot water came from the tap. And there was a lavatory upstairs. And carpets. And something called an eiderdown. And clean sheets. This was all very odd. And rather scaring.

C Food Facts, published by the Food Ministry (1940).

Oatmeal, one of the finest foods for giving warmth and energy, is a 'must' for growing children. They will probably like it as oat-cakes.

Encourage your children to eat baked potatoes, jacket and all. The jacket has a delicious sweet flavour and provides valuable roughage.

Carrots are an important protective food. Most children love carrot when it has been washed, lightly scraped and grated raw into a salad or sandwich.

Never waste the peel and cores of your apples. Boil them in a little water, and you'll have a delicious and very health-giving drink.

D One newspaper described how Devon children were spending their holiday in 1940:

[The children] are covering a wide range of useful tasks – protecting windows against blast, removing ration coupons for the local grocer, tidying the village street, darning socks for soldiers, looking after babies, carrying meals to the harvest field, making signalling flags for soldiers, and digging tank-traps, cleaning Home Guard rifles, thatching a hayrick, sheep-dipping, hoeing turnips, driving cattle, milking and dairy work, harvesting.

The children have [collected] over 4000 lb of bones and an incredible amount of metal, rags, jars, bottles, tinfoil, paper, and cardboard; the aluminium alone filled five sacks.

E From the King to schoolchildren:

8th June, 1946

To-DAY, AS WE CELEBRATE VICTORY, I send this personal message to you and all other boys and girls at school. For you have shared in the hardships and dangers of a total war and you have shared no less in the triumph of the Allied Nations.

I know you will always feel proud to belong to a country which was capable of such supreme effort; proud, too, of parents and elder brothers and sisters who by their courage, endurance and enterprise brought victory. May these qualities be yours as you grow up and join in the common effort to establish among the nations of the world unity and peace.

George R.I.

1 List all the precautions which were taken in case (a) the Germans bombed Britain and (b) they landed in Britain.
2 a) Look at evidence A. Write down the three objects the child is carrying.
   b) Explain why each item was needed.
3 a) Look at the upper drawing on page 44. Which foods were not rationed?
   b) Evidence C gives two ways of saving food. What are they?
   c) What other food, that might be wasted, could people have used?
4 a) Read evidence D. List the jobs which the children did, apart from farming jobs.
   b) Explain why at least five of these jobs were necessary.
5 a) Read evidence E. What 'hardships and dangers' might pupils have suffered?
   b) What hardships did other people suffer?
   c) Which would you have found worst? Give reasons for your choice.
6 Draw your own propaganda poster either to stop people wasting food or to encourage them to buy fewer clothes.

15   Towards the Welfare State

At last there is a saint on earth;
An angel he would be
If only he could have his will
And make the Commons pass his bill.

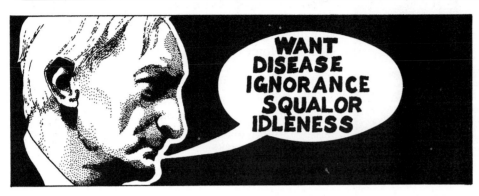

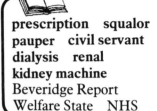

prescription   squalor
pauper   civil servant
dialysis   renal
kidney machine
Beveridge Report
Welfare State   NHS

Beveridge said that these five giants stood on the road of progress.

Even before the war was over, people were thinking about what they wanted Britain to be like afterwards. No one wanted people to suffer again, as millions had in the 1930s. So the government asked Sir William Beveridge to draw up a report. It was published in 1942.

What he said, in the middle of the war, was that the country had to fight another war when it was over. It would be a war against poverty.

His plan was for a new national insurance system. Everybody in Britain would pay some money out of their wages to the government. In return, everyone of working age would receive money if they were sick or out of work.

His plan did not end there. There would be pensions for the old, and family allowances to help parents bring up their children. Above all, he recommended a proper national health service, with free treatment and free **prescriptions**. All these benefits would be for everyone; there would be no Means Test to check who should get them.

His report became a best-seller; everyone was soon talking about it. And with good reason. It was one of the most important reports ever written. It has affected the lives of everyone living in Britain today, including everyone in your school, even though today's pupils were not born in 1942.

Beveridge said poverty was caused by:
* unemployment   * illness
* having a large family

His plan was designed to get rid of poverty; instead, people would have security. He planned to give them 'social security from the cradle to the grave'. We call it 'the Welfare State'.

It was a bold idea. Some MPs thought the country could not afford it; others said that Britain could not afford to do without it.

Germany at last admitted defeat in 1945. For five years, Britain had been run by a government made up of the three main political parties. Now, there was a general election and the people chose the Labour Party by a large majority.

A start had already been made on some of Beveridge's proposals. The new Labour government now had to finish the job and satisfy all the hopes which had grown during the war.

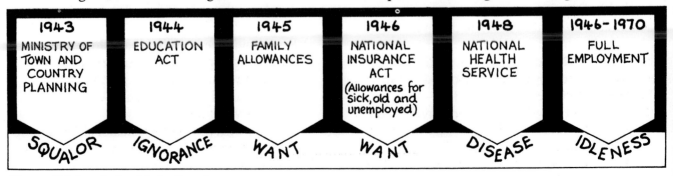

1943	1944	1945	1946	1948	1946-1970
MINISTRY OF TOWN AND COUNTRY PLANNING	EDUCATION ACT	FAMILY ALLOWANCES	NATIONAL INSURANCE ACT (Allowances for sick, old and unemployed)	NATIONAL HEALTH SERVICE	FULL EMPLOYMENT
SQUALOR	IGNORANCE	WANT	WANT	DISEASE	IDLENESS

How politicians dealt with the five giants.

A This article appeared in *Picture Post*, 1943.

WHAT A MINISTRY OF SOCIAL SECURITY WOULD MEAN TO THE ORDINARY CITIZEN

Picture Post, March 6, 1943

What happens to-day to an individual who meets with misfortune : an extreme case to illustrate the maze through which Beveridge has **pointed out a clear, simple way.**

1 *John Jones, a man of 64, finds that he has fallen out of work through no fault of his own.*

2 *He draws unemployment pay: at this point his case is dealt with by the Ministry of Labour.*

3 *After 26 weeks he is no longer entitled to the dole and is turned away to go elsewhere.*

4 *He has now to go to the Assistance Board. Here he applies for the unemployment help he needs.*

5 *The first of many investigators arrives at his home—this time from the Assistance Board.*

6 *He falls ill. Unable to work, he is no longer able to get help from the Assistance Board.*

7 *A new investigator arrives—from the Approved Society, which now deals with his case.*

8 *Still another investigator—from the local Public Assistance Committee, to which he has had to apply.*

9 *His 65th birthday present: a visit from a fourth investigator—to look into his pension claim*

Wife Falls Ill
Son Steals
MEANWHILE
Child is Ill
All Mean More Investigators

A MINISTRY OF SOCIAL SECURITY WOULD COMBINE ALL THESE FUNCTIONS

John Jones when he falls out of work has plenty of trouble besides the gnawing anxiety about his family's welfare. He is passed from one set of officials to another until he feels like an official form worn out by constant stamping. How absurd that a fresh investigation has to worry him whenever he suffers a new misfortune, that there is no single set of papers about him and his family for everybody to consult! When he comes to the end of his road—an old age pension— he reaches the crowning absurdity: at this point his case actually comes under **Customs and Excise!** It is this state of affairs which a **Ministry of Social Security** would cure. John Jones **would** go to one local office for all his claims; there **would be** one set of papers about him and one investigator to help and advise. And the people working in this office would not treat him as a wrong-doer, but as a man fallen on evil times who must be lifted up again.

B An extract from a Ministry of Information film of 1941. A young soldier is talking to an older one. (They were played by actors.)

We've been doing some hard thinking lately and we haven't got to stop when this job's finished. There'll be work enough, too, when this lot's over, building up something new and better than what's been destroyed. There mustn't be no more chaps hanging around for work what don't come. No more slums, neither. No more dirty filthy back streets and no more half-starved kids with no room to play in. We've got to pack all them up and get moving out into the brightness of the sun. We've got to all pull together.

C A letter from Vita Sackville-West to her husband, an MP, in December 1942:

I hope that [the Beveridge Report] gets whittled away. I am all for educating the people into being less awful, less limited, less silly, and for spending lots of money on (1) extended education; (2) better-paid teachers, but *not* for giving them everything for nothing, which they don't appreciate anyhow.

Health, yes. Education, yes. Old age pensions, yes, I suppose so . . . But not this form of charity which will make people fold their arms and feel that they need have no enterprise since everything will be provided for them. It is surely [an] error.

1 Copy out and complete this paragraph:
Sir William _____ published his Report in _____. He recommended a new national _____ system to provide 'social security from the _____ to the _____'. In the general election of 1945, the _____ Party was elected to carry out these proposals.

2 a) Write down each of Beveridge's 'five giants' on separate lines. Beside each, explain what you think the 'giant' was.
b) What solution did he suggest for 1 and 5?
c) What solutions can *you* suggest for the other three?

3 a) Look at evidence A. Why might the man's wife and son be ill?
b) Why might his son steal?
c) How does this article suggest that things would be better under the Beveridge plan?
d) Do you think this article is biased? Give reasons for your answer.

4 Read the remaining evidence. Would you have been for or against the Beveridge Report? Give full reasons for your decision.

The National Health Service

Poor family with sick child in about 1900.

For nearly half of the 20th century, most sick people had to pay to get better. True, there were some charity hospitals, and **paupers** who lived in workhouses got free treatment. After 1911, so did workers in the government's insurance scheme. But even they had to pay if their wives or children fell ill. Many families dreaded getting a doctor's bill. They could not afford it.

The Labour government intended to introduce a free national health service (NHS). The man with the job of doing it was the Minister of Health, Aneurin Bevan. He had started work, at the age of 13, in a Welsh coal-mine, for about 50p a week; he had seen how poverty affected the sick.

Bevan's plan was for the government to pay each doctor for every patient on his or her list. People would be able to register with any doctor they wished. They would get free treatment, in or out of hospital, free medicine and dental care. It would be free to everyone.

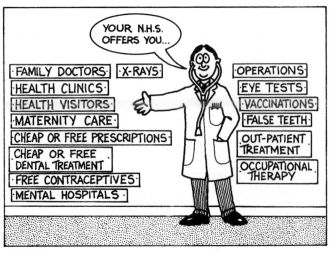

At first, many doctors objected. They were afraid that they would be turned into **civil servants**.

Hospital staff were less of a problem. They knew most hospitals were run-down and badly needed expensive new equipment. Government money seemed the only solution. But Bevan had to agree that doctors could go on treating private patients, who would pay for their treatment.

Of course, all this cost money. All workers would have to pay for the service through taxes and national insurance contributions. When you get a job, you'll be paying, too.

No one really knew how much it would all cost, although about £140 million was estimated. But, when the NHS began in July 1948, there was a flood of patients. People had been 'saving up' their illnesses to get free treatment. Within two years, the service was costing £350 million.

Foreigners were impressed by the NHS.

The cost was – and is – the NHS's main problem. It did not stay wholly free for long. Some charges were introduced in 1951 and, today, there are charges for prescriptions, hearing aids, dental treatment and so on. (However, children and people on low incomes still get these free.)

Another problem is the long waiting lists for free hospital treatment. (There is no waiting if you pay.) Part of the reason is that doctors can cure so many more illnesses now than they could in 1948.

Transplant operations, for instance, have become common. But they are very costly. So is machinery, such as a **kidney machine**. Sometimes, doctors know that they *could* cure people – but there just isn't the money to do so.

However, the NHS was a great achievement. No one can doubt how valuable it has been to millions of people. No one today has to suffer just because they can't afford a doctor.

Evidence A to D is from *The Guardian*, January 8th and 9th, 1985:

A Some 2500 people need life-saving kidney **dialysis** treatment every year. The National Health Service has the facilities to treat about 1400 of them. In an ideal world, the mismatch would be solved by spending more on **renal** services. But this isn't an ideal world. All the health regions are falling short to some degree.

B Doctors at an Oxford hospital have cut off the kidney dialysis treatment which a 44-year-old man needs to stay alive, on the grounds that his life is not of sufficient quality. Yesterday, Mr Derek Sage, who lives in a hostel for the homeless in Oxford, was taken to a private hospital in London for treatment at the expense of a charity.

C Dr Des Oliver, who made the original decision to end treatment, which was later backed by two colleagues at the hospital, felt that Mr Sage should never have been accepted for treatment.

He said, 'He is mentally defective . . . and did not fit the criteria for dialysis. He has progressively deteriorated in that he became virtually mute and unable to look after himself. He became abusive and he was not looked after properly. We had to feed him and he had to be cleaned up. He hit other patients. He hit staff.'

D Politicians, of course, accept rationing [of treatment], whatever party points they make about the efficiency of the NHS. The public largely does so, too. Instant treatment is associated with the private, not the public sector.

E The President of the British Kidney Patients Association said:

Decisions not to treat kidney patients are being taken by doctors all the time. Usually the patient does not understand that he could have been treated and goes away to die quietly.

F This cartoon about the start of the NHS was printed in 1948:

DOTHEBOYS HALL

"It still tastes awful."

1 Some of these statements are true; others are false. Write down the true ones, then explain what is wrong with the others.
   a) The NHS began in July 1948.
   b) It was started by a Liberal government.
   c) Everyone pays national insurance contributions to help pay for the NHS.
   d) All hospital treatment is free.
   e) The NHS guarantees immediate treatment for anyone who needs an operation.

2 a) Look at the lower drawing on page 48. List the benefits of the NHS.
   b) Which two do you think are most important?

Give reasons for your choices.

3 a) Look at evidence F. Who is the man on the left? Who are the men on the right?
   b) What is written on the bowl and why were the doctors having to take this 'medicine'?

4 a) According to evidence C, why was this man's treatment stopped?
   b) The rest of the evidence suggests another reason. What is it?
   c) Which evidence is opinion? Give reasons.
   d) Does this evidence support or contradict the last sentence of the text? Give reasons.

MORE EFFICIENT
ALLOWS BETTER PLANNING
PRODUCTION FOR NEED
ENSURES MORE
EQUAL DISTRIBUTION
AVOIDS WASTEFUL
COMPETITION

Arguments in favour of nationalisation.

The Labour government believed that Britain's major industries should be taken over and run by the state. This policy is called nationalisation. The Labour Party believed it was wrong for owners and **shareholders** to profit from important industries; they should benefit everyone.

From 1946 to 1950, many key industries and services were nationalised. It was an expensive task. Some of these industries needed huge investments to bring them up-to-date. The railways were a good example of this.

UNDER NEW MANAGEMENT

BANK OF ENGLAND 1946
COAL MINES 1946
RAILWAYS, CANALS, ROAD TRANSPORT 1947
ELECTRICITY 1947
GAS 1948
IRON AND STEEL 1949

GREAT BRITAIN LTD

These were all nationalised.

Before the First World War, there were over 120 different railway companies, each running its own lines. During that war, the government took them over. When they went back to private ownership in 1921, they were mostly put into just four groups, to try to meet the competition from road transport.

shareholder rural
nationalisation 'the Beeching Axe'

They tried hard. Many lines around London were electrified. New, streamlined engines were built and trains went faster than ever before. But the age of the motor car had arrived. After the railways became nationalised in 1948, a lot of money was need to bring them up-to-date.

Diesel engines, as well as electric trains, soon replaced steam engines. Diesel engines are cheaper and easier to look after. But still the new British Railways lost money and some lines were closed.

THESE WERE PRIVATISED

BRITISH AEROSPACE
BRITISH TELECOM
WYTCH FARM
CABLE AND WIRELESS
AMERSHAM INTERNATIONAL
SEALINK FERRIES
JAGUAR CARS
BRITOIL
BRITISH RAIL HOTELS
SCOTT LINLITHGOW

After 1979, the Conservative Party followed a policy of privatisation. This meant selling back industries to private ownership.

In 1963, Dr Beeching became Chairman of British Railways and produced a report about the state they were in. His solution was to cut losses by cutting lines. He planned to close down many minor lines which lost money; 2000 stations would be shut and sold.

His plan was nicknamed 'the Beeching Axe' and there were bitter arguments about it. Villagers were afraid they would be cut off; people without cars would not be able to get about so easily.

A few small lines escaped Dr Beeching's 'Axe' but thousands of kilometres of track were closed. Even so, British Rail has gone on losing money. It is a problem facing most railways in the world in this age of mass motoring.

A Route distance on Britain's railways. (This does not include sidings or extra parallel tracks.)

1900 – 35 164 km	1950 – 31 296 km
1910 – 37 629 km	1960 – 29 555 km
1920 – 38 188 km	1970 – 19 464 km
1933 – 32 583 km	1980 – 17 641 km

Note: the figures from 1933 onwards do not include Southern Ireland.

B From an article in the *Sunday Times*:

It is said that British Railways are losing £300 000 every day. No doubt we ought to be disturbed by this information. But what touches the heart more deeply is that our Railways are losing at least one more Line every year; one more unpunctual but peaceful journey; one more chance for the traveller to watch the scenery of his countryside.

C One signalman told a reporter:

Twenty-four thousand quid a year they paid Beeching to close the lines. I'd have done it for £2000 and been laughing. There's coal lorries come past my house, shaking it to bits, and a disused line runs past the back garden. If it was me, I'd say all right, never mind about the passengers, they've all got cars – but anything over five tonnes, on the railway, boy.

D In 1938, Mallard set a record of 201 kph for steam locomotives. It has never been beaten!

E From Dr Beeching's Report, 1963:

Stopping services developed as the main form of **rural** public transport in the last century. The only alternative was the horse-drawn vehicle and private transport of any kind was very limited. Even in those days, many of them failed to pay.

Today, rail stopping services and bus services serve the same purpose. Buses carry the greater part of the passengers moving by public transport in rural areas. Both forms of public transport are fighting a losing battle against private transport.

In 1938, the number of private cars was 1 944 000 and in 1961 there were 6 000 000. In addition, in 1961 there were 1 900 000 power-driven cycles.

1 Explain each word in the word box.
2 a) Which industries were nationalised?
   b) Choose two of them and explain why they were so important to Britain.
   c) What reasons have been given for nationalising industries?
   d) Write down any disadvantages which you think nationalisation may have.
3 a) Using evidence A, draw a block graph to show how the railway system has changed.
   b) Why do you think there was such a drop from 1960 to 1970?

4 Read the rest of the evidence.
   a) Is evidence B and C for or against the Beeching Plan? Give reasons.
   b) Which one gives the best reasons? Explain how you decided.
5 Divide your page into two columns, using a pencil and ruler. On the left, write down any arguments for closing lines which lost money. On the right, write down the arguments against it. On balance, do you agree or disagree with what Dr Beeching did?

17 Housing

Little boxes, on the hill-side,
Little boxes made of ticky-tacky,
Little boxes on the hill-side,
Little boxes all the same.

In 1900, many people lived in dreadful slum houses. The First World War made things even worse. But Lloyd George promised people afterwards that the government would build 'homes fit for heroes'. After 1919, it started doing just that.

Local councils were told to build houses and the government provided cash to help them. Unluckily, money was short in the 1920s and 1930s and many schemes were less successful than they might have been.

Clearing the slums was a slow business but the councils did build over one million new **council houses**. Yet over 2½ million private houses were built between the wars. **Mortgages** were cheap; if you had a good job, a house was easy to find.

The housing problem which faced the Labour government in 1945 was huge. No houses had been built during the war; about 20 per cent of existing houses had been damaged or wrecked by bombs. House prices were three times what they had been during the war.

council house   mortgage
prefab   New Town   high-rise flats

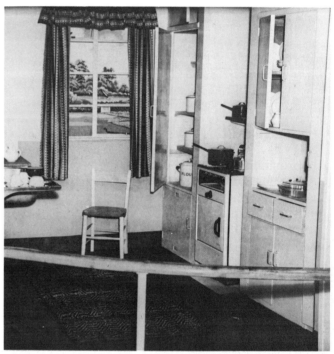

The up-to-date kitchen of 1949.

Homes were needed fast. One emergency solution was to put up 'prefabs'. These were one-storey buildings which were made in factories. The pieces were put together on the site. They were supposed to be used for just ten years but some are still lived in.

Another idea was to build whole new towns in the countryside. The idea was to re-house people from the slum areas of older towns. Unlike most towns, these were properly planned from scratch.

The government did have problems, such as a shortage of building materials. Yet, by 1950, Britain had built more new homes than any other European country. Even more were built in the 1950s, but it was still not enough.

People in general were becoming better-off and wanted a home of their own, just when the population was rising. Land was getting scarcer. So house prices rose.

A Liverpool slum in 1933.

House prices kept rising.

The planners had to look for other solutions. As building land was expensive, one obvious answer was to build upwards. The result was tall blocks of flats, called 'high-rise' flats.

But these new flats were unpopular with many residents. Young mothers and old people easily became lonely in them; often, there was nowhere safe for children to play; in some cities, whole blocks were wrecked by vandals.

In any case, many were just not safe, though no one knew that when they were built. A block which cost £4 million to build might cost £11 million to repair.

Despite rising house prices and the higher cost of mortgages, more people still bought their own homes, rather than rented them. This trend increased when the Conservative government encouraged council house sales after 1980.

High-rise flats in London in 1961.

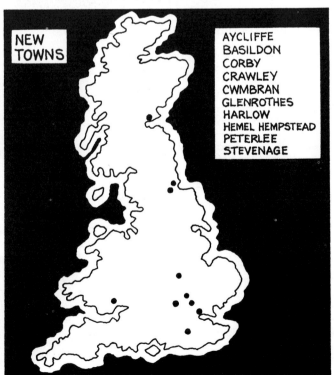

NEW TOWNS

AYCLIFFE
BASILDON
CORBY
CRAWLEY
CWMBRAN
GLENROTHES
HARLOW
HEMEL HEMPSTEAD
PETERLEE
STEVENAGE

1 Explain the meaning of each of these words: council houses; prefabs; high-rise flats.

2 Which of the pictures on these two pages are evidence? Give reasons for your answer.

3 a) Draw the map on the left.
b) The new towns are named beside the map. Using an atlas, name each town on the map.
c) If you were planning a new town, which of these things would you provide: houses; flats; factories; shopping centre; pubs; dance hall; offices; airport; station?
Give reasons for your choices.
d) What else do you think is needed?

4 a) Look at the picture of the slum on page 52. What were the disadvantages *and* advantages of living there?
b) Look at the high-rise flats above. What are the advantages and disadvantages of living in such a block?
c) What are the risks of each kind of housing?

5 a) Look at the kitchen picture. What do you think was attractive about this in 1949?
b) How is it different from a modern kitchen?

18 Education

Come hither, Master Michael Tylles,
And into their heads we'll hammer
Godly Learning to guide their wills,
Arithmetic, Writing and Grammar.

In 1900, all children under 12 had to go to school, but few stayed beyond that. Parents had to pay to keep older children at school and many needed their children to get a job and earn money.

In 1902, the government decided to encourage secondary education which local authorities were given the job of providing. They still do, today.

But only 25 per cent of children went to a *separate* secondary school. These children went to a **grammar school** until they were 16 or 18 and their parents paid fees. However, there were now more free places for poor children. Other children stayed in their **elementary schools** until they left.

When the slump came after the war, many plans had to be dropped. But the government knew that most older children were getting a poor deal. So they set up a committee to look into education.

The result was the Hadow Report of 1926. What it suggested was a major change – and it was one which still affects many of you today. It said that primary education should end at 11. Older children should go to secondary schools.

grammar school   elementary school
11-plus examination

In some parts of Britain, children are still 'selected' in this way at 11. But most teenagers now go to comprehensive schools. These are designed for all young people, whatever their interests and abilities.

A few of these were built in the 1940s and 1950s. Then, in 1965, the Labour Government asked all local education authorities to make plans for them.

At every major change, some people have complained. But perhaps that is not so surprising. After all, everyone goes to school now for at least 11 years. It is the one subject about which everyone has some experience – and their own views!

During the Second World War, people began to plan for the future. In 1944, a new Education Act said that secondary education should be free, like primary education. In the last year of primary school, pupils would have a test to decide the kind of school they would attend after 11. After going through secondary school, they could go on to further education at 15, if they wished.

Time	Monday	Tuesday	Wednesday	Thursday	Friday
9.00	French	Geography	English	English	History
9.45	Prayers	Prayers	Prayers	Prayers	Prayers
10.00	P.T.	Geography	French	History	French
10.45	R.I.	English	Maths	French	Maths
11.45	History	Latin	Geography	Maths or English	Biology
12.30	History	Latin	Geography	Maths	Biology
1.15	Lunch	Lunch	Lunch	Lunch	Lunch
2.20	Maths	Science	Games	Latin	Cadet Force
3.00	English	Science	Games	Latin	Cadet Force

A school timetable for third-year boys (1960).

54

A Charlie Chaplin spent some time at an orphans' school after 1896:

Punishment took place every Friday in the large gymnasium. [At] the far end, behind a long school desk, stood the [offenders] waiting for trial and punishment. On the right and in front of the desk was an easel with wrist-straps dangling, and from the frame a birch hung ominously.

For minor offences, a boy was laid across the long desk, face downwards, feet strapped and held by a sergeant, then another sergeant pulled the boy's shirt out of his trousers and over his head, then pulled his trousers tight.

Captain Hindrum, a retired Navy man weighing about 200 pounds [90 kg], stood poised, measuring [the cane] across the boy's buttocks. Then he would lift it high and with a swish bring it down across the boy's bottom. The spectacle was terrifying, and invariably a boy would fall out of rank in a faint.

The minimum number of strokes was three and the maximum was six. If a culprit received more than three, his cries were appalling. The strokes were paralysing, so that the victim had to be carried to one side.

B Roald Dahl described punishments at his school between the wars:

[The Headmaster] used to deliver the most vicious beatings to boys under his care. At the end, a basin, a sponge and a small clean towel were produced by the Headmaster, and the victim was told to wash away the blood before pulling up his trousers.

C *TV Times* carried out an opinion poll in 1983. They asked, 'Do you approve of corporal punishment?' These were the results:

In Favour of Corporal Punishment:

Pupils 62%   Parents 81%   Teachers 54%

D A classroom in about 1900:

E A modern classroom:

1 a) Draw a time-line for the years 1900 to 1990. Use 1 cm for each ten years. Mark these dates on your time-line: 1902; 1926; 1944; 1965; 1972.
   b) For each date, write down what happened in that year and why it was important.
2 Look at the left-hand drawing on page 54. Do you think all children fall into one of these groups? Give reasons for your answer.
3 a) Is the timetable on page 54 evidence or not?
   b) Do you think it gives the lessons at a grammar, technical or modern school?
   c) What are the main differences between this timetable and the one which you have?
4 a) Read evidence A and B. Do you think the writers were for or against corporal punishment? Explain how you decided.
   b) Look at evidence C. Why do you think fewer teachers than pupils were in favour?
   c) How might it have been different 70 years ago?
5 a) Look at evidence D and E. List the differences between these scenes.
   b) How are the children different – and why?

19 The 1950s: from Austerity to Affluence

prosperity   hire purchase   recession
consumer society   productivity
austerity

The Labour government had done much to rebuild Britain – and create the Welfare State – despite the problems it faced. It had followed a policy of austerity. This meant strict controls over industry and people. Shortages in the shops meant people went without things they wanted so that more goods could be exported.

Rationing continued and, in 1948, rations were actually cut below war-time amounts. Even bread had to be rationed. Meanwhile, prices went on rising.

At the 1951 general election, Britain elected a Conservative government, led by Winston Churchill. The Conservatives were to stay in power for the next 13 years. For most people, these were years of growing **prosperity**. There was full employment and people had more money to spend.

At the same time, there was more to buy. Washing machines and fridges had been luxuries: now they became common. Even cars and television sets were not just limited to the rich. Shops encouraged people to spend by offering **hire purchase** arrangements.

'Most of our people have never had it so good,' said Harold Macmillan in 1957. And most people agreed. They saw the government's main job as trying to improve living standards and Macmillan won the 1959 general election.

Britain had become a **consumer society**. However, there was a problem. From 1955 onwards, Britain was regularly buying more goods from abroad that it was exporting. More money was going out of the country than was coming in.

A A party poster from the 1959 election:

We want a Britain where production expands year by year and the growing wealth is fairly shared throughout the nation

When Labour came back to power in 1964, it found that Britain was spending £750 million more abroad than it was earning.

Living standards went on rising during the 1960s but Britain was already falling behind countries such as America and Germany. Their **productivity** was higher than in Britain; they were more successful at selling abroad; and their living standards were higher.

These economic problems remained a major worry for every government in the 1970s and 1980s. Macmillan was right when he said that Britain had 'never had it so good'. But most people were too busy enjoying it to notice that other countries were having it better.

1945	1950	1955	1960	1965	1970	1975	1980	1985
LABOUR	CONSERVATIVE			LABOUR	CON.	LABOUR	CONSERVATIVE	
Attlee	Churchill	Eden	Macmillan / Douglas-Home	Wilson	Heath	Wil-son / Callag-han	Thatcher	

The governments and Prime Ministers of Britain from 1945 to 1985.

B Publicity handout from the 1959 election:

I'm voting   because...

as a housewife with a family to look after, I'm doing all
right with the   There's so much more in
the shops. And I've got more to spend too. Ever since
the   took over our standard of living has
gone up and up. I don't want any more Socialist
'experiments.' I'm going to stick with the

Vote

C Cartoon showing Harold Macmillan as 'Supermac' in 1958. (Transport House was Labour Party HQ.)

"I TOLD YOU THIS SORT OF STUFF WILL FETCH 'EM BACK INTO THE OLD CINEMA . . ."

D Enoch Powell was a Conservative MP at the time. In 1971, he said:

Harold Macmillan still saw, as in the 1920s, unemployment and **recession** as the true enemy, always waiting round the corner. Thorneycroft* more correctly, it has proved, saw inflation as the post-war enemy and saw as the central issue the maintenance of a stable value for money. He was prepared to postpone other desirable objects of government [for this]. (*Thorneycroft was Chancellor of the Exchequer. He resigned in 1958 because he wanted to reduce government spending. Macmillan disagreed.)

1 Copy out and complete this paragraph:
   The Labour government after 1945 had followed a policy of _____. There were _____ in the shops and _____ continued. In 1951, _____ became Prime Minister. The 1950s were years of growing _____ for most people. Shops encouraged spending by offering _____ _____ arrangements.
2 a) Draw the time line on page 56.
   b) Which party has been in power longest?
   c) Which party has not been in power?

3 a) Look at evidence C. Do you think the cartoonist was for or against Macmillan?
   b) Try to work out: (i) why he calls him 'Supermac'; (ii) why the cinema is called the TORYTZ; (iii) why the 'film' is a U Certificate.
4 a) Look at evidence A and B. Write down which one you think was produced by Labour and which was produced by the Conservatives. Explain how you decided.
   b) Read page 56 again, then design a poster for the 1959 election for the party of your choice.

A This man visited villages, selling sheet music in the 1890s, before the days of pop music. (The first British Top Ten did not appear until 1955.)

B Fashions in the 1950s.

Look for:
full skirt

seamed stockings
bobby sox

jacket with velvet
collar
tight trousers

wide belt

man's 'Brylcreemed'
hair

The Birth of Pop Music

The arrival of pop music was one sign that young people were better off. There had been popular music before the 1950s, but it was *everyone's* music. The pop songs of the 1950s onwards were mainly for teenagers. For the first time ever, young people had their own music. It was rock'n'roll.

Many older people said it was just a passing craze. But, instead of dying, the craze grew. There were even riots in cinemas showing rock films! Teenagers welcomed the music not just because they liked it. It had an extra appeal: adults *didn't* like it.

Rock'n'roll music was a kind of rebellion against older generations. People were beginning to see teenagers as a separate group; a generation gap was opening up between young and old.

Yet, oddly, the first rock hit was 'Rock Around the Clock', sung by Bill Haley, who was at least ten years older than his fans. But he was soon followed by many young singers. One soon became more successful than all the rest – Elvis Presley. People even called him 'the King'.

His TV and stage appearances shocked adults; his wriggling hips even earned him another nickname – Elvis the Pelvis! Yet, today, his records, like most others of the time, sound very mild. They were mainly sentimental songs about teenage love.

By the 1960s, pop music had found new subjects. Singers like Bob Dylan were recording 'protest' songs which were a direct attack on the older generation and its beliefs. The younger generation was now expressing its views on all sorts of social and political issues.

But the leading singers were still mainly American. It was the arrival of the Beatles in 1962 which made British pop music popular throughout the world. They were soon millionaires and were even awarded the MBE by the Queen. Pop music was becoming 'respectable' with older generations.

Yet some groups still represented the rebellious side of youth. *The Who* smashed up guitars on stage; and *The Rolling Stones* shocked many people by openly using drugs. A decade later, the *Sex Pistols* made records which tried to shock older people. New Wave rock groups of the 1970s tried to rediscover the excitement of the early years of rock music.

But the fact that such groups could exist at all was due to the pioneers of the 1950s. They created the demand for pop music; later groups have had a ready-made audience.

58

C Fans at a Beatles concert in 1963:

D An Australian newspaper reported in 1955:

Press agent Ben Reyes boasted today that he had organized the mobbing of Johnny Ray by Australian fans. Johnny's suit was a 'breakaway job'. 'It was made to fall apart if you breathed on it,' Reyes said. 'But the Aussies were very polite, and I had to send one of our boys to start pulling it to give the natives the idea.'

E Ex-Beatle Paul McCartney, said in 1984:

There'd be a lot of screaming, rather than like nowadays, people are a little bit more reserved. It was never as crazy as they used to say it was. If you'd see a bunch of kids coming towards you, you could stop them. They'd only want your autograph; and you could chat.

The thing about fans [was] I used to do the same thing myself. I felt like I understood what they were on about. Some people who didn't understand what they were on about thought they were coming to get them and ran. So Johnny Ray and people like that would run and they'd rip his jacket off.

F Elvis Presley in 1956.

G An American missionary was quoted in 1976:

I've seen naked savages, jungle dancers; I can't see the difference between what our young people are doing around the world in rock and roll dancing. It all [came] out of the jungles and I think rock and roll is taking us all right back to the jungles today.

I think Elvis Presley and the Beatles and the Rolling Stones are going to answer to God for all the pollution of youth around the world. All this rock culture is just stirring people up to do evil instead of to do good. Just as the people were doing in Noah's day. Just look at their dress and the glasses they wear. God is going to rain judgment upon earth and there will be a time when all hell will be let loose on earth.

1 This chapter covers the history of the first 25 years of pop music. In one or two paragraphs, write your own history of pop music since 1980.

2 a) Do you think the man in evidence A sold songs to younger or older people?
b) How can you tell that the people in B are quite well-off?
c) How can you tell that photograph B was not taken in 1900? (At least two reasons.)

3 a) Look at evidence F. Why do you think this sort of act shocked older people?
b) What does it make you think?

4 Read the rest of the evidence.
a) Why did the press agent claim that the suit was made to fall apart?
b) Do you believe him? Give reasons.
c) Do you think Paul McCartney has read evidence D? Give reasons for your answer.
d) Describe the reaction of the fans in C.
e) Do you think McCartney is right when he says that people are more reserved today?
f) Would you behave like the fans in C?
g) Do you agree or disagree with evidence G? Give reasons for your answer.

20 Radio and Television

This wonderful age goes to show
That all the world is a stage.
First, you heard; now, you see
And you wonder what the next thing
On the list will be.

Pop music has affected most young people around the world but some other new kinds of entertainment have affected all generations.

In 1900, people either went out to be entertained or stayed at home and entertained themselves. For instance, they sang and played the piano.

Today, more and more people stay at home to be entertained. This great social change began with gramophones and radios; and it has grown since the invention of television and video-recorders.

The 20th century began with the radio. In 1901, its inventor, Marconi, sent a radio message across the Atlantic. In 1920, the Marconi Company experimented with broadcasting from Chelmsford. It was followed by the British Broadcasting Company in 1922. (This is now the British Broadcasting Corporation, or BBC).

By 1939, radio was an important part of national life. Nine out of ten British families owned one. When the Second World War started, Chamberlain told everyone in a radio broadcast.

However, by then, television had begun. It was invented in 1926 by John Logie Baird, but the BBC chose a different system when they began regular TV broadcasts in 1936. By 1939, there were still only about 20 000 sets in use, compared with about 9 million radios.

The television service shut down during the war years and did not really become popular until the 1950s. Sets were cheaper by then and, in 1955, Independent Television (ITV) started, so viewers had a choice of programmes.

BBC2 followed in 1964 and Channel 4 in 1982. Meanwhile, colour programmes had begun in 1967. Television had become the most popular form of entertainment.

The effect has been huge. Many theatres and cinemas were forced to shut down. There was less point in paying to see stars when you could watch them on television for nothing.

Above all, television has made the world seem a smaller place. In 1962, the satellite Telstar brought the first live pictures from America; in 1969, viewers watched live pictures of American astronauts on the moon.

But it is also easy to sit 'glued to the box' and limit your world to your living-room!

1 a) Write the following dates on separate lines, in chronological order: 1955; 1901; 1926; 1964; 1936; 1962.
   b) Beside each, write what happened then.
   c) What do you think is the most important of all events since 1950? Give reasons.
2 a) Read evidence A. What are the main differences between programmes then and now?
   b) Why do you think there were many news broadcasts during the General Strike?
3 a) Look at evidence D and E. Write down at least four ways in which BBC programming changed between 1961 and 1984.
   b) Suggest reasons why it changed.
   c) Do you think it got better or worse by 1984? Give reasons for your choice.
4 a) Read evidence F. Do you think the writer is correct? Give reasons for your answer.
   b) If this does happen, how will it change people's lives?

TV sets were expensive just after the war!

A During the General Strike there were regular radio news bulletins. These were the radio programmes for May 5th 1926:

London – Call 2LO (36 metres) – 10 a.m. News. 1 p.m. Time; News; Orchestra. 3.15 – Schools. 4. – Time; News; Talk. 5.15 – Children. 6. – Orchestra. 6.50 – Gardening Notes. 7. – Time; Weather; News; Talk. 7.25 – Claude Briggs (piano). 7.40 – Wireless Association Talk. 8. – Opera by Purcell. 9.30 – Weather; News; Talk. 10. – Extracts from the revue, 'Bubbly'.

B Listeners took radio very seriously. Here, an actor described how listeners reacted to a serial he was in:

For some, *Mrs Dale's Diary* was real. We all got an immense amount of fan mail, but a lot of it was really about the characters we were playing. Mrs Dale was asked to [get] medical advice from her husband. When Gwen was pregnant she received lots of little gifts for 'the baby'. And when the dog died, people even sent in wreaths for the grave.

C Watching TV in the 1930s. The screen measured 23 cms:

D Breakdown of BBC TV programmes, 1960–61:

Opera, music and ballet	2.0%
Religion	2.5%
Outside broadcasts (other than sport)	2.5%
Miscellaneous	4.0%
School broadcasts	5.3%
News	6.4%
Drama	7.4%
Films	8.0%
Light entertainment	11.3%
Children's programmes	12.0%
Outside broadcasts (sport)	15.3%
Talks, demonstrations and documentaries	23.3%

Total: 3299 hours

E Breakdown of BBC TV programmes, 1983–84:

Music	0.1%
Religion	2.3%
Continuity	3.2%
School broadcasts	1.2%
News	5.9%
Drama	4.4%
Films and series	18.7%
Light entertainment	6.7%
Children's programmes	12.1%
Sport	12.3%
Current affairs, features and documentaries	27.2%
Continuing education	3.0%
Open University	2.8%
Programmes in Welsh	0.1%

Total: 5881 hours

F In 1973, James Burke predicted:

Flat screen Three-D very soon, certainly. And maybe I'm sticking my neck out, but I think TV will be seen on two levels – one as we have now, the other a sort of information flow. Today, TV's a one-way system. We just look. The 'goggle box.'

In 50 years' time, it could be a two-way communications device, so that you can press a button for the Town Hall to ask about your rates, or switch over to your friends for a game of TV bridge. [A card game.] With cablevision, there'll be hundreds of channels.

21 From Empire to Commonwealth

Wider still and wider
Shall thy bounds be set;
God, who made thee mighty,
Make thee mightier yet.

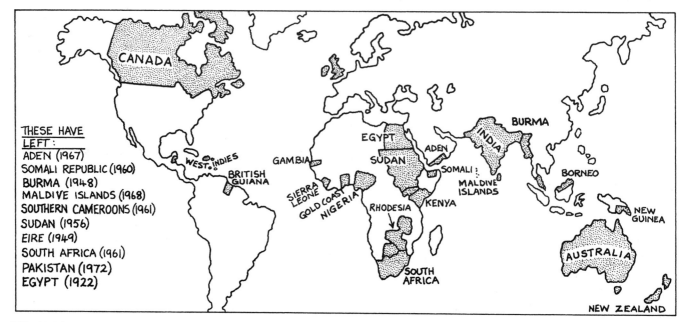

THESE HAVE LEFT:
ADEN (1967)
SOMALI REPUBLIC (1960)
BURMA (1948)
MALDIVE ISLANDS (1968)
SOUTHERN CAMEROONS (1961)
SUDAN (1956)
EIRE (1949)
SOUTH AFRICA (1961)
PAKISTAN (1972)
EGYPT (1922)

The British Empire in 1901.

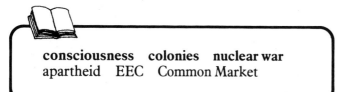

consciousness   colonies   nuclear war
apartheid   EEC   Common Market

When Queen Victoria died in 1901, people from all over the British Empire came to her funeral. It was a great occasion. The greatest Empire the world had ever known was on display. About one quarter of the world's population lived inside this Empire.

When Queen Elizabeth II became queen in 1953, her coronation was also a spectacular event. Representatives from most nations turned up; they included people from the 50 countries in the Empire and Commonwealth.

The word 'Commonwealth' had been used after the First World War to describe the links between Britain and the Dominions – Canada, Australia, New Zealand and South Africa. They had been running most of their own affairs even before the war.

After the Second World War, there were growing demands from many other countries which also wanted to govern themselves. The first to win independence was India in 1947. The British pulled out of the country leaving two new, independent states – India and Pakistan. Of course, others wanted their freedom, too.

In Britain itself, the Labour Party supported those countries which wanted freedom. By the middle 1950s, the Conservative Party, too, accepted that change had to come. In 1957, the first African **colony** got its independence – and a new name: the Gold Coast became Ghana.

In 1960, the Prime Minister, Harold Macmillan, visited Africa. He talked about this new desire for freedom to the South African government. 'The wind of change,' he said, 'is blowing through this continent. Whether we like it or not, this growth of national **consciousness** is a fact.'

The white South Africans certainly didn't like it. They did not want to share power with the blacks; they wanted to keep their system of apartheid. This means keeping the whites and blacks separate. A year later, South Africa left the Commonwealth.

But, elsewhere in Africa, country after country was given its independence. The same happened throughout the world and most of these new nations stayed in the Commonwealth.

62

A In 1982, Argentina attacked the Falkland Islands, one of Britain's last colonies. Armed forces were used to recapture it and 255 servicemen died. Defending the islands is still an expensive job.

B This was the shield of Achimota College in the Gold Coast. It showed the keys of a piano. An African explained what it meant: 'You can play a tune of sorts on the white keys and you can play a tune of sorts on the black keys, but for harmony you must use both the black and white.'

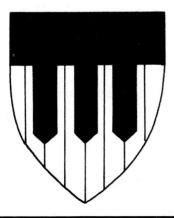

This change did have problems. In some countries, such as Kenya, there were riots. But, on the whole, it succeeded. The Empire became the Commonwealth – an organisation of independent, free countries.

In any case, another change was taking place. In the past, most of Britain's trade had been with the Empire. In 1950, about half of all British trade had been with the colonies.

By 1962, Britain was selling more to Europe than to the Commonwealth. Britain's economy was pulling her into closer ties with Europe.

In 1957, six European countries had joined together in the European Economic Community (the EEC). Usually, people just call it the Common Market. The idea was to co-operate on trade; many leaders hoped this would lead to greater agreement and unity in Europe.

Britain had stayed out. But most politicians believed that Britain's trade would increase if she joined the Common Market. If this happened, the extra trade would mean more jobs in Britain and a higher standard of living.

1 Each of these sentences contains a mistake. Write each one out correctly.
   a) In 1953, Elizabeth was crowned Elizabeth I.
   b) The Commonwealth has become the Empire.
   c) India became independent in 1974.
   d) Harold Macmillan described the independence movement as 'the wand of change'.
2 a) Draw the outline of the map on page 62.
   b) Using a modern atlas, name the members of the Commonwealth. Use their modern names.
   c) Shade in those countries which have left the Commonwealth.
3 a) Look at evidence B. What do you think the African meant?
   b) Design your own badge (or flag) to show how different peoples can work together in peace.
4 Discuss what Britain could do with her remaining colonies. Would you (a) give them independence; (b) give them to other countries; (c) keep them under British rule? Work out what the problems would be for *each* solution. Can you think of any other ideas?

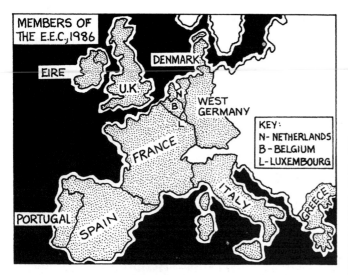

MEMBERS OF THE E.E.C., 1986

EIRE
DENMARK
U.K.
N
B
L
WEST GERMANY
FRANCE
PORTUGAL
SPAIN
ITALY
GREECE

KEY:
N - NETHERLANDS
B - BELGIUM
L - LUXEMBOURG

In 1973, Britain at last joined the Common Market. To bring Britain into line with Europe, she began using the metric system. The change-over is still not complete.

Nor is it yet clear how successful the Common Market is really going to be. Its members often argue, especially over the price of food. And attempts to bring members together politically have hardly started.

There have been disagreements inside the Commonwealth, too. Many people think it still has not proved its usefulness. Unlike other world organisations, it has no rules; it is a loose organisation of states which try to help each other whenever they can.

Throughout history, it has always been more difficult to bring countries together in friendship than to bring them together to fight a war. Only time will tell whether, with the Commonwealth and the Common Market, this time the politicians have succeeded.

But, today, they have to live with a greater threat than ever before. The war they wish to avoid could, next time, be a **nuclear** one.

1 a) Draw the map shown above.
b) In what way is Britain different from every other member?
c) Do you think this is important or not?
2 Look at the column on immigration.
a) What can (i) the Government and (ii) ordinary people do to stop race riots?
b) Do you agree or disagree with the speaker in evidence B? Give full reasons for your view.

Immigration

After the Second World War, many people from Commonwealth countries came to Britain to live and work. Britain needed workers and some even had their fares paid. At first, most came from the West Indies; by the 1960s, there were also many immigrants from India and Pakistan.

However, by then, there was less need for new workers. The Government passed Acts in 1962 and 1968 which limited the number of people allowed into Britain each year.

Some found they were abused or even attacked, often because of the colour of their skin. There were race riots in some cities, such as London and Bristol. Others settled in more easily and brought their own culture to the areas they lived in.

A The Notting Hill Carnival, which is organised every year by West Indians in London:

B One immigrant said on television in 1971:

A million and a half black people on the sidelines. That is what you have. All they need black people for is to produce whenever they want them to produce. Apart from that, you stand on the sidelines, rotting, dying, festering. The question is – Whose responsibility it is to pull us off the sidelines and involve us into the society. I believe that to involve us would mean serious changes in the society itself.

Revision

In 1941, the magazine *Picture Post* printed 'A Plan for Britain'. It described some of the things which it thought Britain needed. These were the headlines it used for some of its ideas:
Work for All; Social Security; A Plan for Education; Health for All; A Real Medical Service.

a) Put these in what you think is their order of importance. The most important one will come top of your list.

b) Under 'A Plan for Education', it said:

* The same kind of education for all up to 13
* The child's future education to be decided at 13
* The public schools brought into the general system
* Some Youth Service for everybody
* A break between secondary school and university

a) Which of these things have not happened?
b) Is there anything you disagree with in this list? If so, give reasons.

2 Below are outlines of 5 famous people of 1900 to 1970, along with some things they said. Your job is to work out who is who. In your book, write each quotation on a separate line. Beside each, write the name of the person who said it.

'I WAS CRAZY ON FLYING.' · 'THE WIND OF CHANGE.' · 'HOMES FIT FOR HEROES' · 'VOTES FOR WOMEN' · 'SOCIAL SECURITY FOR ALL'

3 This is how one woman spent one week at some time in the 20th century. She kept this record at the time. She was aged 29 and her husband was in the army. Read it through carefully before answering these questions. (There are plenty of clues.) For each answer, explain how you decided.
a) Did she live in the town or country?

b) Roughly when do you think she wrote this?
c) What modern equipment would she not have had?
d) How would you expect a modern housewife's week to be different from hers?
e) Ask an adult in your family to write down how they spend their week. Are there any differences you did not include in (d)?

	Morning	Afternoon	Evening
Monday	7.15 a.m. Get up. Have breakfast. Do some of own household duties. 9 a.m. Go out to work. 1 p.m. Finish	Have a cup of something to drink. Do some more of own housework. Feed chickens. Call and make Uncle's bed. Clean the Reading Room. Fetch Library Book.	4.30 p.m. Tea. Go to Uncle's, light fire, do odd jobs. Feed cat and dog. Wash. Knit, read, or listen to wireless. Supper and to bed. Read a little in bed and smoke a cigarette.
Tuesday	7.15 a.m. to 1 p.m. Same as Monday.	1 p.m. to 4.30 p.m. Same as Monday, except no Library. Do the washing, finish about 7.30 p.m.	Write letter. Knit, read or listen to wireless until 9 p.m. Cigarettes and a glass of Guinness perhaps.
Wednesday	Same as Monday.	1 p.m. to 4.30 p.m. Same as Monday, except no Library and no Reading Room. Visitor to tea (Relation).	6 p.m. to 10 p.m. Out to work. Bed. Read a little. Smoke a cigarette.
Thursday	Same as Monday.		7 p.m. to 9 p.m. Work at home. Bed. Read and smoke.
Friday	Same as Monday.	Same. Clean Reading Room.	7 p.m. to 9 p.m. W.E.A. class. Supper, bed, read and smoke.
Saturday	Same as Monday. 1 p.m. Dinner.	Go to Uncle's and work there until about 5.30 p.m. Tea at home.	Read and knit. Listen to wireless. Bath and to bed later than usual. Read and smoke in bed. Do not feed chickens on Saturday.

22 Nuclear Weapons

Tell the leaders of the nations,
Make the whole wide world take heed;
Poison from the radiations
Strikes at every race and creed.

Gives Britain influence in the world.

They protect Britain against nuclear attack.

So horrible that no one dares use them.

Encourages others to get nuclear weapons.

They could not protect us against nuclear attack.

There is no defence if one is dropped.

Arguments for and against the bomb. Background picture shows Hiroshima after it had been bombed.

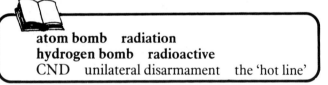

**atom bomb   radiation
hydrogen bomb   radioactive
CND   unilateral disarmament   the 'hot line'**

On August 6th 1945, the United States dropped an **atom bomb** on the Japanese city of Hiroshima. About 70 000 people died; many others who survived died later from the after-effects of **radiation**.

What America began, others soon took up. In 1949, the Russians tested their first atom bomb; British tests in the Pacific followed in 1952; in 1957, the British were testing their first **hydrogen bomb**.

By then, scientists had begun to learn about the after-effects of these bombs. Amongst other things, they found that tests added **radioactive** chemicals to the atmosphere. People throughout the world began protesting at the manufacture and the testing of these bombs.

In 1958, British opponents formed themselves into a group called the Campaign for Nuclear Disarmament – CND, for short. They believed that Britain should give up the bomb completely, without waiting for other countries to do so. This policy is called 'unilateral disarmament'.

At Easter 1958, CND organised a march from Trafalgar Square to Aldermaston in Berkshire. Aldermaston is an atomic research centre.

Protests were organised again in 1981 when American Cruise missiles were to be based at Greenham Common in Berkshire. Many women who were against nuclear weapons set up a camp outside the base. In 1987, the United States and Russia agreed to destroy nuclear missiles like these.

One other change has taken place since the 1950s. In 1963, the USA, Russia and Britain signed a Nuclear Test Ban Treaty. There would be no further tests in the atmosphere, although underground tests could still go on. However, France and China did not sign the treaty and each carried out atmospheric tests in later years. South Africa, Israel and India now have nuclear weapons, too.

Also in 1963, a direct telephone link was set up between Washington and Moscow. It is called the 'hot line'. The idea is that Russian and American leaders can get in touch easily. People hoped that it might perhaps stop a future war.

A Two survivors at Hiroshima:

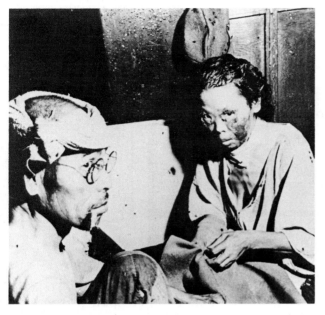

B In 1957, Aneurin Bevan told Labour supporters who wanted unilateral disarmament:

You will send a Foreign Minister, whoever he may be, naked into the conference chamber. Able to preach good sermons, of course; he could make good sermons. But action of that sort is not necessarily the way in which you take the menace of this bomb from the world.

C An author described Dr Teller, a nuclear scientist, in 1984:

He is against locking up a scientific secret for the same reason that he is against banning a nuclear bomb test. He still believes deep in his soul that science is good, that the spread of scientific knowledge can only be good, and the spread of its products also.

D James Cameron, a reporter, wrote in 1967:

By 1963 it was possible to say that one phase of the Campaign for Nuclear Disarmament was over; that the first stage of its purpose was complete. It had been, after all, unique. It had done more than teach people to think about the Bomb; it had taught them how to think. Great numbers of people in peculiar clothes made themselves uncomfortable and suffered in prison for demanding a Test Ban – and by and by there was a Test Ban.

The CND was one of the good things in a discouraging world; it earned its place in the records, and with honour.

E The estimated effects of a one megaton explosion on Bristol, showing the radioactive fallout:

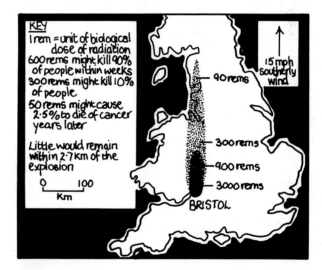

1 a) Write each of these dates on separate lines, in chronological order: 1958; 1949; 1945; 1952; 1963.
   b) Beside each, write down what happened in that year.
2 Look at all the evidence on this page.
   a) Why did Aneurin Bevan argue against unilateral disarmament?
   b) Was writer D for or against the bomb? Explain your answer carefully.
   c) Write down any facts contained in evidence B, C and D.
3 What do you think would happen if:
   a) Britain scrapped all her nuclear weapons and banned others from coming in?
   b) All countries banned nuclear weapons?
   c) Britain got more nuclear weapons?
4 Look carefully at the different views shown at the top of page 66.
   a) Can you see anything wrong in either side's arguments? If so, explain what it is.
   b) What is *your* view? Remember to give reasons for your answer.

23 Law and Order

CHANGES IN THE PRISONS...

1920s — CONVICT HAIR CUTS ENDED

BROAD ARROWS ON CLOTHES REMOVED

1974 — BREAD AND WATER DIET ENDED

probation
open prison
capital punishment
treason birched
juvenile court
borstal

The 20th century has seen major changes in law and order. Police today have more equipment to catch criminals and new ways of getting information. Television cameras and computers help police to track down criminals; so, too, do walkie-talkies, police dogs and police cars.

But there has been change of another kind, too. In the 19th century, criminals were mainly treated as wicked people who simply deserved to be punished. The 20th century has seen great efforts at reforming criminals.

It began in 1907 when the government passed an Act allowing criminals to be put on **probation**, rather than sent to prison. In the next year, children were tried for the first time in their own juvenile courts.

The first borstal for young offenders had already opened at Borstal in Kent in 1902. In 1961, short-term imprisonment was stopped for people under 17. By then, some adult prisoners were also getting different treatment. The first **'open' prison** was set up at Wakefield in 1937.

Prison reforms continued after the war. After 1962, no prisoner in England was **birched** as a punishment. And, after 1965, **capital punishment** was abolished for murder, but not for **treason** or piracy with violence.

Yet the crime rate, for most kinds of crime, went on rising. This was partly because more people lived in bigger cities than ever before. In country areas, there are fewer crimes – and more of them are solved.

By the 1980s, existing prisons were full to bursting point and the government was having to plan more. The problem of crime and of what to do with the criminals is not a new one, but the 20th century has not yet solved it.

...AND FOR THE POLICE

1901 — FINGERPRINTS FIRST USED

1909 — BICYCLES...

1919 — ...AND THE FLYING SQUAD

1923 — TWO-WAY RADIOS

1967 — BREATHALYSER TESTS

A Crimes recorded and cleared up, 1978–82:

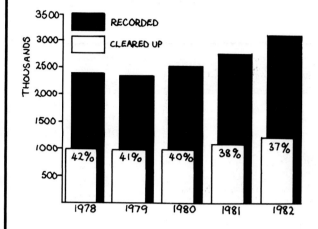

C One of the first women police wrote in 1918:

Our street is one of the worst streets in London. So I am informed and certainly I hope that there are not many that could be called worse. Since the 'Women Police' have worked there, a big difference has been noted and commented on by [various people. They include] a ragamuffin of about 15 years, too early initiated with the evils of the world, yet of a sunny, unspoiled [nature]. He is the great champion of the Women Police Service.

'Don't you carry a truncheon?' he asked me one day; 'I bet yer does.' 'What should I do with a truncheon?' I [asked]. ''it 'im on the 'ead,' was the reply given with great relish.

D In 1919, many policemen went on strike because they wanted to join a trade union. These policemen were from London.

B The kind of crimes committed in 1982:

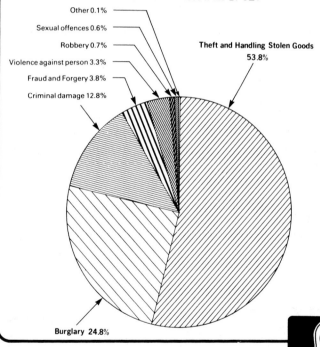

1 Match up the dates on the left with the correct event on the right:

1902	the first 'open' prison set up
1907	breathalyser tests started
1934	capital punishment was abolished
1965	probation system began
1967	first borstal was opened

2 a) Look at evidence A. What proportion of crimes were *not* solved in 1982?

b) What else can you work out from evidence A?

3 Give your own opinion on these questions. In each case, give reasons for your answer.

a) Do you agree with the youth in evidence C?

b) Do you think police should be allowed to go on strike?

c) What would happen if police did strike?

d) Which crime was most common in 1982?

e) Why has the crime rate kept increasing?

f) The Home Secretary is the man responsible for law and order. If you were Home Secretary, what action would you take to reduce the crime rate?

The Swinging Sixties

Mothers and fathers throughout the land
Don't criticise what you don't understand,
Your sons and your daughters are beyond your command
For the times they are a-changing.

affluent   hippies
pirate radio station

A Pop art picture: 'Got a Girl' by Peter Blake, 1960.

Many of the trends which had been happening in the 1950s came to a head in the 1960s. People were describing Britain as 'an **affluent** society' and much of the new wealth went on consumer goods. There were more electrical goods for the home; more people owned their own car; and cheap foreign holidays became common.

Above all, people were attracted to what was young and 'trendy'. In the 1960s, the young had more money to spend so manufacturers began to produce things specially for them.

As a result, young people had their own fashions, dances and pop music – especially *British* pop music. British pop was popular around the world and Britain was seen as the most 'swinging' of countries.

For many young people, pop music became a way of life. 'Pirate' radio stations broadcast non-stop music from ships at sea, until the government banned them. And shops played pop music for their customers, especially for those buying clothes.

But young people showed their taste most clearly in the clothes they wore. Jeans were the most common symbol of freedom, but each year brought some new fashion trend. Skirts grew shorter and shorter until, at one stage, some were only 30 cms long. They were so short that tights came to replace stockings.

While skirts were shorter, hair was much longer, especially among students. And there were more students than ever before because the government had built a number of new universities and colleges.

Some students rejected older people's ideas and a few became **hippies**. They spoke of love and peace, and talked of creating a different and peaceful world. Others turned to drugs, which were illegal but easier to buy than ever before.

The 1960s were a time of rapid change in another way. In 1961, a Russian called Yuri Gagarin became the first man to go into space. Before the decade was over, the Americans had landed men on the moon.

It was a time of experiment – and hope. And it had its effect on the older generations. Parents might have complained about their children but soon they, too, were wearing longer hair and shorter skirts. Even the government accepted that times were changing. In 1969, it reduced the voting age so that everyone over 18 could vote in an election.

In 1963, one vicar banned boys in jeans from his youth club. He said they were liars and thieves.

70

B Fashions of the late 1960s, when girls were often known as 'dolly birds'.

D In 1984, Fred Housego recalled:

The most absurd thing I did in [1967] was I once went out in a pair of bottle-green flared trousers, a bare midriff, a short green crewneck and a scarf. I may look back on it now and cringe at all the silliness but it really was a unique experience to be able to dress and behave like a right haddock and get away with it because everybody else was acting just like a right haddock.

C In 1973, one writer commented:

Between 1961 and 1971, real income per head rose by 29%. Half of all British households now have cars, two-thirds have refrigerators and washing machines, and nine out of ten television sets. Most of the supporters of Edward Heath and Harold Wilson have also never had it so good.

But by the standards of other modern industrial countries, we are being left behind. By 1966, our national income per head was less than that of the Americans, Canadians, Swiss, Swedes and Danes; it had [also] been overtaken by every country in the EEC except Italy.

The blame for the slow growth combined with bad industrial relations, rests on both sides of industry: on management, who will not or cannot make production rise fast enough; and the trade unions, who will not or cannot co-operate effectively in higher productivity.

They prefer to bicker over their shares of the cake instead of joining forces to make the cake bigger. But in this they are merely expressing the general preference of the British people: they 'want it now.'

1 Explain the meaning of each of these words: 'affluent society'; consumer goods; hippies.
2 a) Describe the clothes worn by the woman on the right in evidence B.
b) Now, draw an outline figure of a young person in fashionable clothes today. Use captions to describe the main features.
c) What are the main differences?
3 a) How does writer D look back on the clothes he wore in 1967?
b) Why did he choose those clothes?
c) Think back to something you once wore which you now find silly. Describe it and say why you wore it in the first place.

4 a) Read evidence C. What reasons are given for Britain not getting richer?
b) Whom does the writer blame, and what does he blame them for?
5 Each of the following things shocked many parents in the 1960s: pop music; mini skirts; long hair; drugs. In each case, suggest a reason why.
6 a) After reading the evidence, do you think the text on page 70 gives a fair picture of Britain in the 1960s? Give reasons.
b) Which piece of evidence matters most to us today? Give reasons for your choice.

25 The Changing Place of Women

Come, march with us to victory;
Come, join the battle song,
Of women chained to labour,
Who are suffering grievous wrong.

At Work . . .

Before the First World War, women lived very different lives from those of modern women. Better-off girls did not go out without a chaperone; many of them stayed at home, instead of going out to work. Only one married woman in ten actually had a job and, of course, none of them could vote.

The war changed much of that. Many women had a job for the first time in their lives; it brought them money and independence. Their efforts in the war also helped women over 30 win the vote in 1918. Most professions were opened to women after 1919; so was higher education.

Even so, some jobs were not open to married women before 1939. Most banks, for instance, insisted on employing unmarried women. Some wives even went to work with their wedding ring on a chain round their neck so that their boss would not guess!

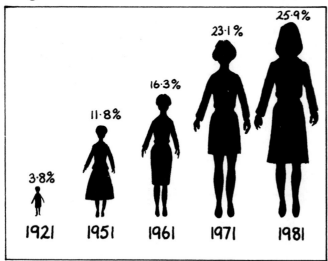

Married women became a larger part of the total workforce.

At the same time, there was greater freedom. Public transport and the motor car gave women independence which would have been unthinkable in Victorian times. Yet none of this brought equality with men.

Although more women were working, few of them earned as much as men in the same jobs. In 1963, women in manufacturing jobs earned an average of £8.40 per week. But men were earning an average of £17.29 a week.

In 1970, the government passed the Equal Pay Act to force employers to pay equal wages to men and women doing the same job. And the Sex Discrimination Act of 1975 ensured that men and women would get equal chances when job-hunting.

These changes were partly due to a new movement which began in the late 1960s. People called it 'Women's Lib', which was short for 'liberation'. It was not only a campaign for equal rights; it was a campaign *against* the way men treated them.

In 1979, Margaret Thatcher became the first female Prime Minister in the west. In 1952, she had said, 'I hope we shall see more and more women combining marriage and a career.'

Despite all the changes, women in Britain have perhaps achieved less than women elsewhere. A larger proportion of women go on to higher education in America than in Britain; Russia has more women doctors.

People have suggested various reasons for this. Some say that it is because most women just do not take advantage of the chances open to them; other people think that girls are still treated unequally, for instance, by their parents or in school. Many people, however, say that it is just too soon for the movement to have had its full effect.

A Cartoon of 1983, published in the magazine of the Equal Opportunities Commission:

B F Sherwood Taylor wrote in 1940:

The majority of women are not artists in home-making. They choose the worst furniture – which is the reason why there is so much of it about; they arrange it anyhow, clean it superficially, and get out of the house as soon as they can. They cook only the simplest meals – frequently from tins, and face the washing-up with a groan.

That the majority of women should spend several hours each day in doing a distasteful job badly is a very serious matter; for they are, after all, human beings. A woman is no more born to be a [servant] than is a man.

C Patrick Jenkin, a Conservative Minister, said in 1979:

Quite frankly, I don't think mothers have the same right to work as fathers. If the good Lord had intended us to have equal rights to go out and work, he wouldn't have created man and woman. These are biological facts. Young children do depend on their mothers.

1 Copy out and complete this paragraph:

Before the First World War, only one married woman in _____ had a job but most professions were opened to women after _____. Progress was slow between the wars, although women over _____ had received the vote in _____. Most women earned _____ than men doing the same job.

2 a) Women gained new rights in 1970 and 1975. In your own words, explain what they were.
b) Which do you think was most important? Give reasons for your answer.

3 a) Look at the figures on the left of page 72. Think of at least two reasons why more women are now at work.
b) What are the advantages for a married woman?

4 Are the pictures on page 72 evidence or not? Give reasons for your answers.

5 Are there any jobs which you think should not be done by *either* men *or* women? If so, write them down and give your reasons.

6 Read evidence B and C. Write a letter to one of these people, giving him your views on what he has said.

. . . and at Home.

Married women gained most from the changes. In 1900, a husband was usually head of the household. His word was law to both his children and his wife. It took a long time for this attitude to die. Even in 1945, many wives told interviewers that they could not say how they would vote in the election until they heard from their husbands.

Contraception probably brought the greatest changes. In 1900, a working-class wife married young and often spent 15 years having babies and bringing them up. The contraceptive pill, invented in the 1950s, allowed women to choose whether they wanted that sort of life.

So, many women chose to spend just a few years having a family, then returned to work. By 1961, there were more married women with a job than unmarried women. In the 1970s, free contraception became available on the National Health Service.

In 1943, Churchill said, 'If this country is to survive as a great power, our people must be encouraged to have larger families'.

Married women gained freedom of another kind, too. In 1900, a divorce was expensive and almost impossible for most women. For many, there was no way out of an unhappy marriage. A number of laws in the 20th century made divorce easier.

The Divorce Reform Act of 1969 especially tried to make divorce a quicker and less painful event. It laid down just one ground for divorce – the complete breakdown of a marriage, for whatever reason. By the 1980s, one marriage in three ended in divorce; one child in eight lived in a one-parent home.

The start of the Open University in 1971 meant that married women could study for a degree at home, while bringing up children. Changes such as this meant that women had far more job opportunities than they did in 1900.

MODERN CONVENIENCES...

FRIDGE   WASHING-MACHINE   TUMBLE-DRIER   ELECTRIC LIGHT   CENTRAL HEATING

COOKER   FOOD MIXER   DISH WASHER   PLASTIC TILES

However, many wives found that having a job brought less freedom, not more. Often, their husbands still expected them to do all the cooking and housework, on top of doing a full-time job.

The 'women's lib' movement helped change these attitudes. Surveys showed that more men were helping to do housework in the 1980s. But, although many men were helping with cooking and washing up, cleaning and hand-washing tended to stay 'women's work'.

In a few families, however, husband and wife swapped roles completely. The husband stayed at home to bring up the children and do the housework while the wife went out to work. Nothing could be more different from people's attitudes in 1900.

...MAKE HOUSEWORK EASIER

BREAKFAST CEREALS   TINNED FOOD   FROZEN FOOD   CONVENIENCE FOODS

FREEZER   WASHING-UP LIQUID   DRIP-DRY SHIRTS

Discuss the evidence before answering the questions.
1 Women's freedom has been increased by (1) being able to get paid work; (2) easier divorce; (3) free contraception; (4) more chances for part-time study.

A Lady Bell described a meeting in 1907:

I was told the other day [about] a young married woman living with her husband and two children on 95p a week. They paid 29p for their home [and] the four of them had 66p with which to pay for food, coals, clothes, absolutely everything, and not one penny more. And somehow this woman actually managed to do it.

A young professional man one day asked the woman how many children she had. 'Two,' she replied. 'And how long have you been married?' 'Six years.' 'Only two children in six years!' he said. '*You ought to be ashamed of yourself.*'

B The Electrical Association of Women did a survey in 1935 of the time women spent on housework:

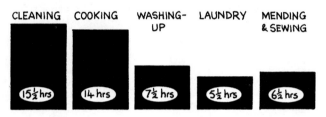

| CLEANING | COOKING | WASHING-UP | LAUNDRY | MENDING & SEWING |
| 15½ hrs | 14 hrs | 7½ hrs | 5½ hrs | 6½ hrs |

C In 1984, one teenager described her feelings about her parents' divorce:

In the eyes of society I am now a member of a one-parent family, but I don't even consider that view. I am still part of the average family; it is just that my dad doesn't live with us. My parents are still as loving towards us now as they were, before the divorce, if not more.

At first, we were harmed by the divorce, but now we realise they could have harmed us more by bringing us up in an atmosphere of hatred and tension. Who knows, perhaps now with divorce being easier, my parents are normal and it's the mum, dad and two children [family] which is becoming a rare breed. Maybe in a few years' time it is they who will be the 'one-in-five' and not us.

D In 1913, Mrs J G Frazer described how a wife without servants should train her family. (By 1975, only one home in 200 had a servant.)

Husbands and children will need much training and teaching by the servantless housewife. But the question is, how can they help her?

Husbands can do much by [not doing things.] The first among these is to refrain from grumbling. Grumbling being abolished once and for all, what next can a man refrain from? Well, he need not splash about in his bath-room like a hippopotamus at the Zoo; he need not throw tobacco ashes or cigarette ends about; he need not scatter his ties.

When he takes off his clothes, he need not expect some female member of his family to see to them the next day. Before going to bed, a well-trained husband empties his pockets, brushes his clothes, folds them neatly, and puts them in their proper place.

E Hal was 13 and Wendy Lou was 15 when they got married in America in 1984. It was only allowed because she was pregnant *and* their parents agreed. Marriage at that age remains illegal in Britain.

a) Explain how each one of these has changed women's lives for the better.
b) Choose the one you think most important. Give reasons for your choice.
c) Write down any disadvantages you can think of.
2 a) What does the writer in C suggest may happen? Do you agree with her?
b) If she is right, how would this affect life in Britain?

3 Read evidence D. Make up your own list of ways in which *either* a husband *or* a son could help a wife today. (Be reasonable!)
4 a) Draw the diagram in evidence B.
b) Ask your mother to work out how she spends her time now. Draw a diagram to illustrate her figures.
c) What differences do you notice between your answers? Suggest reasons for them.

26 Trade Unions

To take away the right to earn a decent living wage,
The furnaces they'll soon be closing down;
The sky no more will glow and six thousand jobs must go
For the men who make the steel in Shotton Town.

picketing   automation
inflation

Trade unions exist to help their members to get better working conditions and higher pay. The more members they have, the stronger they are when it comes to bargaining with employers.

Union membership was growing before 1914 but the First World War gave it a huge boost. Membership was up to 8 million after the war, almost double the pre-war figure. By then, the unions firmly supported the Labour Party. They wanted the Party to stand up for workers' interests in Parliament.

The rise suffered a setback with the General Strike of 1926. In 1927, the government banned general strikes and made it harder for the unions to collect money for the Labour Party. Its income dropped by one-third.

Perhaps more important, the strike had failed and many people just lost faith in the unions. The depression of the 1930s was a further blow: many workers could not afford to join a union.

Union influence increased again in the Second World War when they supported the government's war effort. When Labour won the election in 1945, the unions were in a strong position.

With full employment, they could push for higher wages and better conditions more easily. In the 1950s, annual pay rises became normal. However, this led to higher prices, which led to more pay demands, and so on.

A A symbol of May Day:

The result was inflation. This means that prices kept rising – and money was worth less. For instance, goods costing £1 in 1969 were costing £3.34 by 1979.

THE UNIONS HAVE FOUGHT FOR:

A SHORTER WORKING DAY   BETTER PAY   PAID HOLIDAYS   SAFER WORKING CONDITIONS

B Trade union membership figures (in millions):

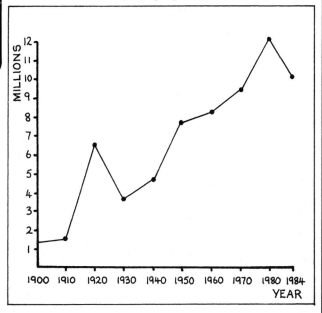

C In the miners' strike of 1984–85, scenes such as this one became common. Police forces in mining areas were strengthened, and miners and police accused each other of violence on the picket lines.

Each Labour and Conservative government tried in different ways to hold down pay rises. In general, the Conservative governments tended to pass laws either to restrict pay increases or the powers of the unions. The Labour Party usually tried to reach a voluntary agreement with the unions instead. Neither solution was successful for very long in the 1960s and 1970s.

In 1974, the Conservative government lost an election after a strike by miners. In its turn, the Labour Party was defeated in 1979 after an outbreak of strikes by various unions.

Mrs Thatcher became the new Prime Minister in 1979. Her policy was to slow down inflation and to restrict the power of trade unions. New restrictions on **picketing** were introduced in 1980.

But the real problem for the unions in the 1980s was rising unemployment. With a smaller membership, unions were in a weaker position to bargain with employers. At the same time, jobs were being lost, often because of **automation**. Fewer workers meant fewer union members. Fewer members meant a weaker union movement.

1 Copy out and complete this paragraph:
   Union membership had gone up to _____ million after the First World War but dropped after the General _____ of _____. The depression of the _____ was another blow to membership. In 1945, the ——— Party won the election and the unions had greater influence.
2 a) Using the figures in evidence B, draw a graph of union membership this century.
   b) Why did numbers drop in the late 1920s?
3 a) Look at the picture in evidence A. Write down what you think is meant by the writing beside numbers 1 to 4.
   b) Of *all* the aims, which do you think are most important today? Give reasons.
4 a) What rights do you think pickets should have? Give reasons for your answer.
   b) If you had been the miners' leader, what would you have told your members?
   c) If you had been the police chief, how would you have advised your men to act?

**Protestant   martyr   patriotic
Sinn Fein   republic**
Home Rule   Ulster   Unionists   Nationalists
'black and tans'   IRA   internment

In the Middle Ages, Ireland was an independent country. Its people were Catholic. In the 17th century, English and Scottish people were settled there to keep the country under their control.

These newcomers were given land which had belonged to the Irish. The settlers were **Protestant** and, by 1700, they owned most of Ireland. But most of the people were Catholic.

In 1801, Ireland became part of the United Kingdom and Irish MPs sat in the House of Commons. The Irish Parliament was abolished. The Irish MPs spent the next century trying to get it back.

By the 1880s, they had managed to convince the Liberal Party that Ireland should be given Home Rule. This meant getting their Parliament again and running most of their own affairs, although Ireland would have stayed in the British Empire. By 1914, Parliament had at last agreed to the idea. Then, war broke out and the plan had to wait.

By then, the Irish people were divided. In Ulster, most people were Protestants. They did not want to be part of an independent Ireland, run by Catholics. They wished to stay inside the United Kingdom, so they were called Unionists.

But many Catholics wanted an independent Ireland without any more delay. Those people who wanted to be separate from the rest of Britain were called Nationalists. They wanted Ireland to be a separate nation once again.

At Easter 1916, some of them organised a rising in the Irish capital, Dublin. They knew they could not win; thousands of British troops outnumbered them. The rising lasted less than a week and hundreds of Irish died.

But its effects lasted through the 20th century. Afterwards, the British shot 15 rebels and this persuaded many Catholics to support the Nationalists. To them, the dead rebels were **martyrs**. Now, they, too, wanted their independence back.

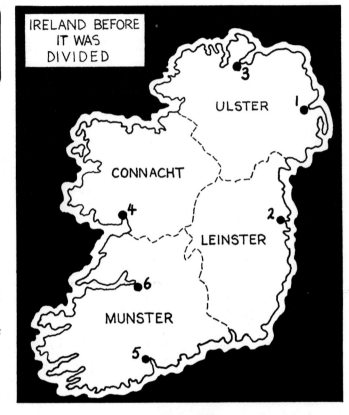

IRELAND BEFORE IT WAS DIVIDED

1 a) Draw the map shown above. Using an atlas, name the places numbered 1 to 6.
b) Why had Protestants gone to Ireland?
c) Give at least one reason why this would have made the Catholics angry.
d) Why did the Protestants wish to stay part of the United Kingdom?
e) Why did Catholics want independence?
2 Look at the picture strip on page 79.
a) Give at least three reasons why the rising was bound to fail.
b) Which of these words do you think describe Patrick Pearse's attitude: proud; hopeless; foolish; determined; brave; **patriotic**; suicidal? Give reasons for your choices.
c) Do you think the British made any errors? Explain your answer.

APRIL 1916 BRITISH SPIES LEARNED THAT A RISING WAS PLANNED.

BUT THE VOLUNTEERS WERE SHORT OF GUNS...

...AND DIVIDED. SOME PASSED THE WORD ROUND THAT THE RISING WAS OFF.

OTHERS DECIDED TO GO AHEAD. PATRICK PEARSE HAD TOLD HIS MOTHER...

THE DAY IS COMING WHEN I SHALL BE SHOT, SWEPT AWAY, AND MY COLLEAGUES LIKE ME.

THEY PLANNED TO SEIZE KEY POINTS IN DUBLIN.

BUT THEY HAD NO ARTILLERY.

AT 12 NOON ON EASTER MONDAY THEY TOOK OVER KEY BUILDINGS.

THE GENERAL POST OFFICE BECAME THEIR H.Q.

THE BRITISH BROUGHT IN TROOPS.

BY WEDNESDAY, THEY OUTNUMBERED THE REBELS BY 20 TO 1.

THE REBELS WEREN'T IN UNIFORM...

...AND BRITISH TROOPS SHOT MANY INNOCENT MALE CIVILIANS...

...AND SHELLED THE POST OFFICE.

BY FRIDAY IT WAS IN FLAMES. THE REBELS ESCAPED AND HID.

5000 BRITISH TROOPS SURROUNDED THEM.

SOME BAYONETED AND SHOT CIVILIANS WHO WERE HIDING.

ON SATURDAY, PEARSE AND OTHERS SURRENDERED.

CIVILIANS BOOED THEM WHEN THEY WERE MARCHED ACROSS TOWN. PUBLIC OPINION WAS MOSTLY AGAINST THEM~ UNTIL...

...THE BRITISH BEGAN REPRISALS. THE LEADERS WERE COURT-MARTIALLED AND SHOT. JAMES CONNOLLY WAS BADLY INJURED. HE WAS SHOT IN A CHAIR.

JAMES CONNOLLY

THE IRISH WERE SHOCKED AT THESE ACTIONS. MANY PEOPLE TURNED AGAINST THE BRITISH. THE BRITISH GOVERNMENT REALISED IT HAD MADE A MISTAKE AND RELEASED MANY THOUSANDS WHO HAD BEEN ARRESTED.

IT WAS TOO LATE. THEY STARTED TO ORGANISE A NEW IRISH REPUBLICAN ARMY (I.R.A)

THIS TIME, THE PEOPLE WERE BEHIND THEM.

JANUARY 1919 IRISH NATIONALIST M.P.'s SET UP THEIR OWN PARLIAMENT IN DUBLIN...

...AND THE FIRING BEGAN AGAIN AT TIPPERARY. THE RISING HAD FAILED ~ YET THE RISING HAD SUCCEEDED ~ AS THE BRITISH SOON DISCOVERED.

The Troubles Continue

After the war, **Sinn Fein** organised the new Irish Republican Army (IRA). It fought a guerrilla war to get the British to leave Ireland. In 1920, the British recruited a new force to support the Irish police.

These were nicknamed the 'black and tans' from the colour of their uniform. They were ex-soldiers and often brutal in the way they dealt with the Irish. On its side, the IRA, too, was committing violent crimes.

The bitter fighting went on until 1921 when each side at last sat down to talks to try to solve the dispute. Some sort of agreement had to be reached. But that was not easy.

The Republicans wanted a united Ireland outside the British Empire. But most of the people in Ulster were Protestant; they wanted to stay part of Britain. The British government wanted to keep them, too. And it wanted the rest of Ireland to stay in the Empire. As this map shows, the British government won.

Yet, in one way, it didn't. Many people in the new Irish Free State would not be satisfied until they had a united, free Ireland. In 1939, the IRA began a bombing campaign in England. Further troubles followed from 1956 to 1961.

By then, the IFS had changed its name to Eire. In 1949, it had become a **republic** and left the Commonwealth.

A turning-point came in 1969. The IRA split into two sections – the Official and Provisional wings. Each wanted the British out of Ireland; the Provisional IRA was – and is – willing to use force to achieve it. Their main methods were public bombings and shooting policemen.

The government in Northern Ireland could not keep law and order so the British government sent in troops. It was to be just a temporary measure – but they were still there in 1986.

Using troops did not solve the problem; in some ways, it made it worse. So, in 1971, the government began internment. This meant arresting suspected terrorists and locking them up without a trial. Still, the violence continued.

So, next year, the Northern Ireland Parliament was closed down and Ulster became ruled directly from London. It still was in 1986. And the bombings and murders continued.

Something else hasn't changed, either. The bitter hatred and distrust still exists between many Catholics and Protestants. Two-thirds of Ulster people are Protestants. Most still do not want to be part of a mainly Catholic Eire.

But many Catholics in Ulster *do* want to be part of Eire; most do not trust Protestants to run their affairs. Somewhere, within all the fear and violence, there lies a solution. But no British government has yet found it.

A The Rev. Ian Paisley, a Northern Ireland Protestant leader, said in 1969:

We are determined in this war never to surrender our Protestant heritage.

B Liam Lynch, IRA Chief-of-Staff, said in 1922:

We have declared for an Irish Republic and will not live under any other law.

C In 1971, this 19-year-old girl was tarred and feathered for going out with a soldier:

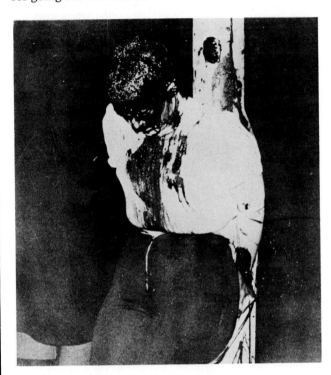

D A Protestant Minister said in 1984:

I would hold that there is no cause which could justify the brutal murder of a young man, a young husband, which can cause his wife to be made a widow and to leave two little children. I don't think there's any cause which can justify that.

E In 1984, a terrorist bomb exploded in the Grand Hotel, Brighton. Leading government ministers, including the Prime Minister, were staying there at the time.

F This woman was permanently scarred by a bomb blast. In 1984, she said:

I see it getting worse. I see violence, bombing. I see a civil war because people aren't going to let it drop. You've got one side fighting for an all-Ireland and the other side wanting to stay with Britain. It's just never going to end.

1 Draw a time-line for the years 1920 to 1980. Use 1 centimetre for each 5 years. On the time-line, mark in what happened on these dates: 1921; 1939; 1949; 1969; 1971; 1972.

2 Read all the evidence.
a) Look at the lower drawing on page 80. Write down each policy and what you think its results would be.

b) For each policy, write down who might object to it.
c) Which policy or policies do you think would improve the situation? Give reasons.
d) Suggest any *other* solution you can.

3 a) Who benefits from the violence? (Think hard!)
b) List those groups which suffer.

In 1967, the Welsh and English languages were given equal status in Wales. Signs such as this one are now in both languages.

executive   manifesto
SNP   Plaid Cymru

Scotland, too, relied on heavy industry. In 1932, one in four Scottish workers had no work. Jobs have disappeared in Scottish coal-mines and in other old industries, such as ship-building. But Scotland gained many new jobs after North Sea oil was discovered in 1970.

But there is another issue which concerns some Scottish and Welsh people even more than employment. It is the feeling that their people, although part of Great Britain, are also a separate people, with their own customs and way of life; each people is a separate nation. These people believe in nationalism.

Each country has its own Nationalist political party which tries to get MPs elected to Parliament. The Welsh National Party began in 1925 and is called Plaid Cymru. The first Welsh Nationalist MP was elected in 1966.

Some of Plaid Cymru's policies.

Very often, school history books hardly mention Wales and Scotland. Yet 8 million people live there and they are very proud of their countries. They elect members of Parliament, just as the English and Northern Irish do.

Welsh and Scottish soldiers fought in the First World War. Afterwards, each country faced a difficult time when jobs were hard to find during the depression of the 1930s.

Wales suffered badly, especially in the South, where coal-mining and iron and steel were major industries. In 1930, in Merthyr alone, 63 per cent of the men had no job. Nearly half a million people left Wales to look for work.

One solution was to build factories to provide new jobs. A few were built before the Second World War; many more were built afterwards. After 1976, the Welsh Development Authority persuaded many foreign companies to begin manufacturing in Wales.

The Scottish National Party (SNP) started in 1934 and its first MP was elected in 1945. It has demanded that Scotland should have its own Parliament to run Scottish affairs.

The SNP has also complained that the profits from oil discovered off the Scottish coast are not spent on Scotland. They feel it is *their* country and that *they* should spend this money on Scotland.

The party symbols. On the left, the Welsh National Party; the SNP is on the right.

Support for these nationalist parties reached a peak in the late 1960s and early 1970s. Although it declined slightly, it has not gone away, any more than the demands of the Irish have done.

In the 1980s, the campaign continued. In 1983, two SNP MPs were elected; and there were two from Plaid Cymru. Many Scots and Welsh still feel that they are Scottish or Welsh first and British second.

1 Copy out and complete this paragraph:
    Many Scots and Welsh people believe that they should have more say in running their countries. Each country has its own _____ party. The Welsh one is called _____ _____; in Scotland, nationalists support the _____ _____ _____ or SNP.
2 a) Read evidence A. Write down four of the SNP's policies.
   b) Look at evidence B. How did the SNP policy differ from that of the Conservatives?
   c) Look at evidence C. What would the SNP have liked in this policy?
3 a) Why do you think people feel so strongly about the country in which they were born?
   b) Why do you think there is no English National Party?
   c) Apart from getting MPs elected, how else could a national party get its policies accepted? Write down any disadvantage for each way you have suggested.
4 Design a poster for either the Scottish or Welsh nationalists. Think of a good slogan to persuade people to vote for you.

A What the SNP said at the 1983 election:

The British political system offers Scotland no hope of improvement. Whichever English party wins the election, regional aid will be redirected to the Midlands of England, to Scotland's disadvantage.

But there is an alternative – to choose Scotland. Never has the need for an independent Scottish Parliament and a Scottish Government been greater.

Only with our own Government will Scotland have the will and the resources to reverse our economic decline and end mass unemployment. Only a Scottish Government will remove all nuclear weapons from our soil. Only a Scottish Government will be able to tackle the appalling social conditions in which many of our people have to live.

B The Conservative Party **manifesto** in 1983 did not make any separate reference to the government of Scotland or Wales.

C What the Labour Party said in 1983:

Labour will:
* Establish a directly elected Scottish Assembly, with an **executive** drawn from members of the Assembly;
* Provide the Assembly with . . . powers over a wide range of domestic policy, including matters such as health, education and social welfare.
* Ensure a major role for the Assembly in assisting . . . Scottish industry . . . within the context of our overall national plan.

The Scottish Assembly will have tax-raising powers, thus ensuring that the level of services provided can be determined in Scotland.

D Welsh holiday cottage destroyed in 1979:

29 Medicine

Coughs and sneezes
Spread diseases.
Trap your germs
In a handkerchief.

Medicine, like so much else, has developed faster in the 20th century than in any earlier one. In 1900, some people in remote parts of Britain were still dressing wounds with cobwebs or cowdung. Today, the NHS offers everyone the latest treatment without any payment.

Partly, people's health has improved because of the National Health Service. But there are other reasons why modern people are healthier than people were in 1900:
* there is much less poverty
* people live in cleaner homes
* they eat better food and have healthier diets
* scientific knowledge is much greater

One major step forward was the wider use of immunisation. This involves injecting a patient with a harmless form of a disease to stop them catching the real thing.

It was used to protect soldiers against **typhoid** and **tetanus** in the First World War. The same method was later used, especially for children, as protection against **diphtheria** and **polio**.

surrogate typhoid tetanus diphtheria polio
immunisation   penicillin

One of the greatest breakthroughs was made by a Scottish doctor, Alexander Fleming. Quite by accident, he found that some mould in one of his specimen dishes had destroyed some germs on which he had been working.

Scientists worked on this mould during the 1930s and it was used in the Second World War to stop blood poisoning. It is still used today; we call it penicillin.

All these improvements have meant that, on average, people live longer than at any previous time in history. In 1900, the average age of death was 46 for a man and 50 for a woman; by 1980, it was 70 and 76 respectively.

The result is that diseases of later life now kill more people than ever. About half the deaths in Britain are now caused by cancer or heart disease.

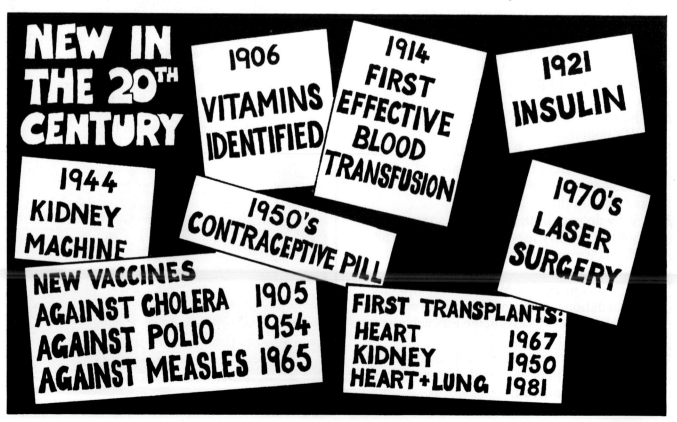

NEW IN THE 20TH CENTURY

1906 VITAMINS IDENTIFIED

1914 FIRST EFFECTIVE BLOOD TRANSFUSION

1921 INSULIN

1944 KIDNEY MACHINE

1950's CONTRACEPTIVE PILL

1970's LASER SURGERY

NEW VACCINES
AGAINST CHOLERA 1905
AGAINST POLIO 1954
AGAINST MEASLES 1965

FIRST TRANSPLANTS:
HEART 1967
KIDNEY 1950
HEART+LUNG 1981

A The operating theatre at Charing Cross Hospital in 1901:

B An operating theatre in 1981:

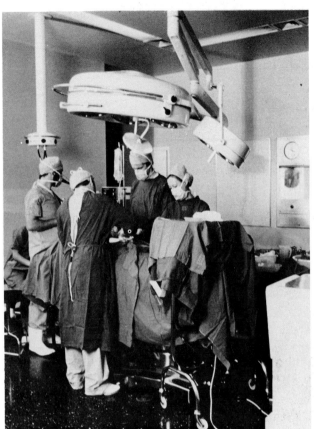

Because people are better off, they have more money to spend on cigarettes and drink; more of them own cars; and an increasing number of young people are drug addicts. The century has seen so many health problems solved; but new ones keep appearing.

FIRST TEST-TUBE BABY BORN ~ July 1978

FIRST BABY BORN TO SURROGATE MOTHER ~ January 1985

£13,000

1 Write one sentence about each word in the word box.

2 a) Give three reasons why people live longer.
b) Suggest another reason which is not mentioned on page 84. Give reasons for your choice.
c) In your own words, explain why heart disease and cancer now kill more people.

3 a) Look carefully at evidence A and B. List as many differences as you can see between these two scenes.
b) Explain how each change has made operations safer.

4 Look at the drawing on page 84. Which of these discoveries do you think has been of greatest benefit? Give reasons.

5 Look at the picture on the left. Decide whether you are for or against **surrogate** births. Then, write out a letter to your local newspaper giving your opinions.

30 Sport and Leisure

He's got football crazy,
He's football mad.
The football it has taken away
The little bit of sense he had.

penalised chalet

Still popular in 1900, this entertainment would be thought cruel today. What is it?

People work much shorter hours today than they did in 1900. Before the First World War, a typical working week was 54 hours; by the 1980s, it was down to 40 hours. So people now have far more time to enjoy themselves – and a huge entertainment industry has grown up.

Take sport, for instance. In 1900, most sports players were unpaid. Only football had many professionals. Even so, it caused quite a stir in 1905 when a Sunderland player was transferred to Middlesbrough. Why? They had paid £1000 for him! Today, transfer fees can top £1½ million.

There has been one other major change. In 1900, the upper class and the working class enjoyed very different entertainments. While the rich went to the theatre, the poor went to the music hall; while the rich held dinner parties for friends, the poor went to the pub.

Today, there is less of a difference. The wireless and talking pictures which appeared in the 1920s were entertainments for everyone, rich and poor alike. The spread of television since the 1950s had even greater effect.

THESE WERE NEW...
GREYHOUND RACING 1926
FOOTBALL POOLS 1923
YOUTH HOSTELS 1930

More than anything else, television helped to break down the barriers between people. It has become a major source of entertainment for just about everybody; and a common topic of conversation for all.

At the same time, higher standards of living have meant that millions of people now enjoy pastimes which were once only for the rich.

That goes for holidays, too. In 1900, most people only had free time at weekends and on Bank Holidays. Only the rich could afford the time and money for proper holidays. By 1939, about 11 million people had paid holidays, although they mostly seem to have stayed at home.

However, by then, a holiday industry was beginning. In 1937, Amy Johnson made a guest appearance when the first Butlin's holiday camp was opened at Skegness. For £4 a week, holiday-makers were offered a holiday with everything included and plenty to do if it was wet.

By the 1950s, cheap package holidays abroad were on sale. About 1 million people a year went on holiday abroad in the early 1950s; in 1982, the figure had risen to 14 million. Spain was a popular choice, although travel agents could arrange a package holiday just about anywhere in the world.

...IN THE 20TH CENTURY
TEN PIN BOWLING 1960
DISCOS 1961
BINGO HALLS 1961

A Faster and faster: record times for the men's mile race this century:

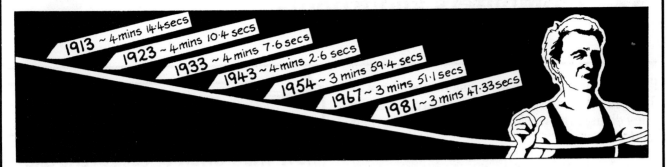

1913 ~ 4 mins 14·4 secs
1923 ~ 4 mins 10·4 secs
1933 ~ 4 mins 7·6 secs
1943 ~ 4 mins 2·6 secs
1954 ~ 3 mins 59·4 secs
1967 ~ 3 mins 51·1 secs
1981 ~ 3 mins 47·33 secs

B How young people aged 15 to 24 spent their spare time in 1979, according to an opinion poll:

Men	%	Women	%
Pub	52	Dancing	54
Pop music	50	Going out with partner	53
Playing sports	48	Parties	50
Going out with partner	47	Friends	50
Friends	43	Pop music	47
Parties	43	Shopping	38
Dancing	38	Pub	38
Attending sports	35	Reading	35
TV	30	TV	35
Cinema	27	Walks	34
Reading	25	Radio	31
Radio	22	Playing sports	28
Walks	20	Cinema	26
Theatre/concerts	16	Theatre/concerts	19
Cards	13	Attending sports	18
Classical music	11	Cards	11
Shopping	6	Classical music	10
Church	4	Church	6

C A magazine article of 1946 about a Butlin's holiday camp:

My friends K3 and K4 were having everything provided for them. This code number represented a typical family, who were being checked through at the camp reception office which everybody refers to in army slang as 'Admin.' They collected a number for their **chalet**, a number for their dining-room position, a number for their luggage and a name for the house they were going to belong to during their stay.

The members of [a] house eat together, play together and compete against other units in such competitions as the knobbliest knees, the camp 'lovely' and the mass keep-fit exercises. The house captain, a member of the Butlin staff, is chosen for his jollity and talent as a mixer. At frequent intervals [he] rallies his house over the camp radio with such calls as 'Hi-di-hi.' The house responds 'Ho-di-ho.' Mr Butlin denied a newspaper report that if a camper refuses to respond he is **penalised**.

A smile on everybody's face is the Butlin motto, and they walk through the camp smiling, even when there's gravel in their shoes and they have heard that one about the elephant for the tenth time that day.

1 Answer the following questions in complete sentences:
   a) What was a typical working week before the First World War?
   b) What were the popular entertainments in 1900 for (i) the rich and (ii) the poor?
   c) What effects has television had?
   d) When did Butlin's holiday camps start?
2 a) What kind of entertainment do you think is shown at the top of page 86?
   b) Is the picture evidence? Give reasons.
3 a) Would you have enjoyed the kind of holiday described in evidence C?
   b) What do you think the reporter's attitude was? Explain how you decided.
4 a) Write down the ten pastimes you most enjoy, with your favourite one at the top.
   b) How does it differ from evidence B?
   c) Suggest reasons for the differences between women and men in evidence B.

31 Computers and Robots

Throughout human history, one thing has not changed. Human beings were, and are, inventors. They change the world around them to suit their needs.

It began about half a million years ago when people made the discovery which made them different from all other animals. They started using tools.

In the 20th century, people are still inventing; they are still making new tools with which to control the world. Only, today, they are so much more complicated. Whereas early people made stone scrapers, modern people design robots and computers.

This is not as new as some people think. The principles which computers use were first worked out in 1823 by a British mathematician, Charles Babbage. He suggested a machine driven by steam!

However, the first electronic computer (the kind we now use) did not appear until 1946, in America. It was huge! It was as big as a house and used as much electricity as a small factory.

Some experts thought there could never be more than a handful of computers in the whole of Britain. You know how wrong *they* were!

These experts thought their use would be limited because they would generate heat and waste energy. The early ones did. The first one had 18 000 valves and got very hot.

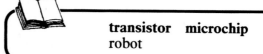

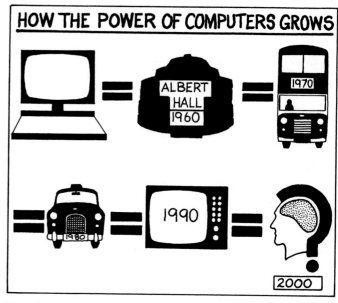

How big a computer had to be to have the same power as a human brain.

The invention of the **transistor** in 1948 solved this problem. **Microchips** were a new solution of the 1970s. So computers grew smaller and smaller – but more and more powerful. Today's experts expect that this will go on happening.

From computers, it is only a short step to robots. A robot is a machine which can do a job on its own. Robots which can carry out human tasks have already arrived.

They don't have brains; instead, they have computers. So they are programmed to do certain jobs; some are also programmed to make their own decisions. By 1984, one British car factory was using 220 of them; they cost £650 million. The result? The firm needed to employ 2500 fewer people.

Some people believe it is a sign of what is to come: more computers, more robots and fewer jobs for human beings. But human beings need jobs to earn money. They need money to live. As Britain enters the computer age, will there be enough jobs to go around? If not, what are we going to do about it?

What a computer looked like in 1950.

A How the cost of computer memory has fallen. These figures give the cost of one page of information (one page = 350 words):

	Working memory	Back-up memory
1950	£1 million	not available
1960	£30 000	£5000
1970	£5000	£1000
1980	£100	£6
1985	£3	30p

B In 1984, Professor Edward Fredkin looked forward to the year 2050:

There's an excellent chance that these very big and fast computers will have been programmed eventually to become intelligent. If they become intelligent, they won't just be intelligent like us, they'll be different. Their intelligence will be a kind of super-intelligence in many ways, but they won't be humans.

I believe that, if that happens, then they will be like another species on this planet. We won't talk to them much because we won't understand what they're doing or why. They will probably, I hope, leave us alone and we will co-exist.

I think it is inevitable. We don't know when it will happen. It's very clear it's the next step in evolution.

C Robot from the film *Undersea Kingdom* (1936):

D The percentage of people unemployed in Great Britain since 1945:

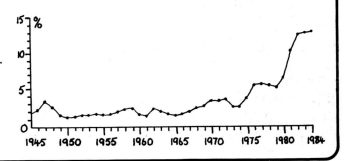

1 Which of the pictures on page 88 are evidence? Give reasons for your choice.
2 a) Why did some experts think that computers would always be rare?
   b) Why is this no longer a problem?
3 a) Read evidence B. Do you think the Professor was right in thinking these developments are 'inevitable'? Give reasons.
   b) What two results does he expect?
   c) What are the dangers if he is right?
4 a) What differences have computers made to your life? (Think hard!)
   b) What differences do you think they will make for you in the future?
5 If there are fewer jobs, these are some possible ways of dealing with the situation:
   i) Accept that many people won't have jobs;
   ii) Allow people to share jobs by working 2½ days a week each;
   iii) Make everyone stay in full-time education until 18 (or 21);
   iv) Introduce a 4-day week for everyone.
   a) What are the advantages and disadvantages of each solution?
   b) Which solution do you think would be the fairest for everyone?

Queen Victoria died in the first month of 1901. She left behind a country that was proud, powerful and confident about the future. Britain exported more goods than any other country; her navy was the world's biggest; her Empire was the greatest the world had ever known.

Nearly a century later, Britain is a very different country. The Empire has gone; by 1985, Britain's merchant navy was only eighth biggest in the world and she was the fifth largest trading nation.

British people played a major part in winning two World Wars, but each one left Britain weaker. Today, Britain is not such a great power. She can no longer compete on a military level with the major super-powers, Russia and America.

Perhaps the most striking change has been in how Britain defends herself. In 1901, Britain felt so secure that she had no allies. But she has long given up 'going it alone'. Since the Second World War, Britain has relied more and more on America: American troops, armed with American weapons, are now based in Britain to help protect British people.

dictator
NATO   privatisation   SDP

AVERAGE ANNUAL INCOMES		
	1900	1976
BRITAIN	£43	£1966
FRANCE	£35	£3244
GERMANY	£30	£3572 *
ITALY	£17	£1508

*WEST GERMANY

LIFE EXPECTANCY IN BRITAIN

In 1949, the country became a member of NATO – the North Atlantic Treaty Organisation. It was set up to defend the west in case there was a war with Russia. In 1973, Britain took a further step away from isolation by joining the Common Market. Britain is now governed partly by laws made by the EEC as a whole.

Another huge change has come in living standards. People in general are now much better off than their ancestors in 1901. They work shorter hours and earn more money; they buy more luxuries and live in better houses.

Yet Britain's living standards have not risen as fast as in many other countries. After the Second World War, many other small nations, such as Austria, rebuilt themselves far faster and more successfully than Britain.

The blame for this did not lie with any one group in Britain. Politicians, industrialists and workers all failed to sort out industrial and economic problems in the 1950s and 1960s. Some people think they still have not succeeded.

Queen Elizabeth II on her Silver Jubilee in 1977. The Royal Family kept its popularity. One 1960s survey showed that Prince Philip would be top choice if the country were to have a dictator.

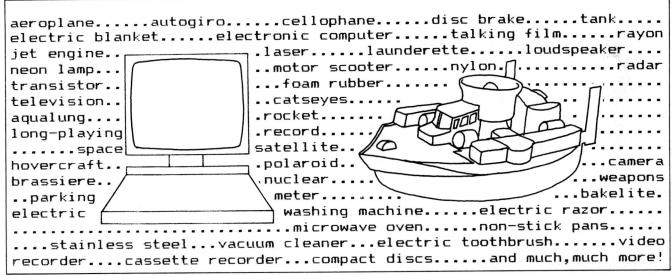

```
aeroplane......autogiro......cellophane......disc brake......tank.....
electric blanket......electronic computer......talking film......rayon
jet engine..                    .laser......launderette......loudspeaker....
neon lamp...                    ..motor scooter......nylon..............radar
transistor..                    ...foam rubber.....
television..                    ..catseyes......
aqualung....                    .rocket.......
long-playing                    .record.....
.......space                    satellite..
hovercraft..                    .polaroid..              ...camera
brassiere..                     .nuclear.....            ...weapons
..parking                       meter.........           ...bakelite.
electric                        washing machine......electric razor......
........................microwave oven......non-stick pans......
....stainless steel...vacuum cleaner...electric toothbrush.......video
recorder....cassette recorder...compact discs......and much,much more!
```

Inventions of the 20th century.

THESE HAVE GONE...

'TREADING WASHING'

WASHING IN STALE URINE

SUNDAY POSTAL DELIVERIES (AND 4 ON EACH WEEKDAY)

PUBS OPEN ALL DAY

TELEGRAMS, POUND NOTES, HALFPENNIES...AND BED-BUGS!

Some writers have argued that Britain has still not got used to being without an Empire. They think that the country has not yet found itself a place in the modern world.

Others believe that the fault lies in the British political system. The voting system means that small parties can get millions of votes, yet only a few MPs are elected. The result has been that the Labour and Conservative Parties have, in turn, run the country.

Very often, their policies are complete opposites. For instance, the Labour Party believes in nationalisation. But the Conservative Party was elected in 1979 with a policy of selling many nationalised industries back to private ownership. It was known as 'privatisation'.

In 1981, the Social Democratic Party (SDP) was founded. It wanted to help the Liberal Party break the two-party system. In the 1983 general election, the SDP won 11 per cent of the votes but only had 6 MPs elected.

...AND THESE HAVE ARRIVED

BRITISH SUMMER TIME (IN WORLD WAR 1)

PAPERBACK BOOKS (FIRST PENGUIN IN 1935)

BALLPOINT PENS (OVER £5 AT FIRST!)

MOTORWAYS (M.1 OPENED IN 1959)

LEGAL ABORTION 1967

NORTH SEA OIL (1970s ONWARDS)

Tradition . . . Change . . . Criticism

The House of Lords still helps to make the country's laws as it did in the Middle Ages. In January 1985, its debates were televised for the first time. One speaker on the first day was the Earl of Stockton, better known as Harold Macmillan. *The Times* reported what he said:

> Let us stop the futile economic arguments and get back to the reality which is happening before our eyes in all parts of the world. You can see more modern forms of production in Taiwan and Korea than you see in England.
>
> It must happen here. We must not be the slowest ship in the convoy. We must be the leader or at least [try] to regain the leadership we have had for so long.
>
> The decision would be for the next generation to make if the country was not to sink slowly like a great ship.

Yet, despite not doing as well as other countries, surveys have shown that most British are very satisfied with their country and their way of life. In one poll in 1974, 85 per cent said they were satisfied with their life. It was the highest proportion of any European country.

One reason may be that, apart from the Irish problem, the nation has had a more peaceful course through the 20th century than most others. There has been no revolution and no **dictator**. Britain has stayed a democracy; nearly everyone over 18 can vote to choose governments. And no one has to carry an identity card which could be inspected by the police.

Each individual's freedom has always been highly prized – and that includes the freedom to criticise the government. There are those who would like to see more rapid change; a few want total change.

More important, each generation has made changes in Britain in the hope that they could improve people's lives. You, too, will seek changes; you, too, will seek to create a better Britain. It is hoped that your understanding of British history will help you to do this wisely and successfully.

BRITAIN IS BEST

I WISH OTHER COUNTRIES REALISED IT

Most British people are proud of their country, according to a 1984 survey.

1 a) Of all the changes mentioned, which one do you think has been most important? Give reasons for your choice.
  b) If you could make one change, what would it be? Again, give reasons for your choice.
2 a) Look at the cartoon on the left. Why do you think so many people are proud of being British?
  b) Are *you* proud of Britain or not? Give reasons.
3 a) Which of these words describe the country you would like to live in: fair; happy; rich; free; caring; strong; equal; safe; powerful; peaceful; contented.
  b) Which words do you think describe Britain today? (You can add others, if you wish.)

Revision

1 Twentieth century crossword. All the answers you need are in this book.

Clues: Across

1. 'n' 5 down! It arrived in the 1950s. (4)
4. _____ Hardie helped to start the Labour Party. (4)
6. His model 7 was a popular family car in the 1920s. (6)
7. Riches from the North Sea after 1970. (3)
8. She has more freedom than in the 19th century, but stays at school until she is 16. (4)
10. Britain is surrounded by it! (3)
12. It warned people of an air-raid. (5)
14. The Test which the unemployed had to face in the 1930s. (5)
16. The Equal _____ Act of 1970 helped women to get fairer wages. (3).
18. The British brought the 'black and _____' into Ireland to deal with the violence. (4)
20. Number 1 or Number 2 or nuclear? (3)
21. Alcock and Brown flew _____ the Atlantic Ocean in 1919. (6)
22. Modern name for the Irish Free State. (4)
23. Many Irish wanted Home _____ in the 19th century. (4)

Clues: Down

1. Machines which do human jobs. (6)
2. One of the first industries to be nationalised. (4)
3. Metric measure introduced since Britain joined the EEC. (5)
4. A ruler, such as Edward VII. (4)
5. See 1 across. The other half of the new teenage music. (4)
9. A woman cricketer might now score one. (3)
10. Nationalist party for Scotland. (1,1,1)
11. Popular female in a Gipsy Moth. (3)
13. Initials of the organisation which wants the British out of Northern Ireland. (1,1,1)
15. There was a General one in 1926. (6)
17. The prisoners lost the broad ones in the 1920s. (5)
18. Jarrow is on this river. (4)
19. First word of SOS. (4)
20. The initials of the organisation which Mrs Pankhurst started. (1,1,1,1)

2 Life has changed more in the 20th century than in any earlier one. But how will things be different in the future? Here is a list of events which may or may not occur.

Computers will replace teachers.
A woman will run a mile in under 4 minutes.
Gas-powered motor cars will be produced.
The Northern Ireland problem will be solved.
The SDP and Liberals will win a general election.
There will be a nuclear war.
Britain will make an alliance with Russia.
Scotland will become independent.

a) Read it through carefully. Decide which event you think is most likely and explain how you decided.

b) Then, write down any other changes which you think will happen. Afterwards, the people in your group can compare their answers to see how much they agree.

Writers and Sources

The derivations of the songs and rhymes used as chapter headings are as follows: chapter 1: music-hall chorus; chapter 2: rhyme which accompanied the *Punch* cartoon on page 11 (1909); chapter 3: topical song about the tragedy by Paul Pelham and Lawrence Wright (L Wright Music Co.); chapter 4: contemporary satirical verse; chapter 5: music-hall song; chapter 6: 'Ain't we got fun' (Feldman, 1921); chapter 7: children's playground rhyme; chapter 9: 'Nice People' (Francis Day/NCB); chapter 10: early 20th-century song (the reference is to cats having been fed on horse-meat); chapter 11: popular song of 1930 (Lawrence Wright Music Co.); chapter 12: 'hymn' sung in Socialist Sunday Schools from 1906 to the tune of 'Auld Lang Syne'; chapter 13: undergraduate lyric to the tune of 'Lambeth Walk' (1938); chapter 14: 'We'll Meet Again', sung by Vera Lynn; chapter 15: verse sent by a senior citizen from Plymouth; chapter 17: modern folk song by M Reynolds (Schroder Music Co., 1962); chapter 18: from a grammar school song of the post-war period; chapter 20: song specially written for a very early BBC TV revue; chapter 21: 'Land of Hope and Glory'; chapter 22: 'H-Bomb's Thunder' by John Brunner, sung after the 1959 CND march; chapter 23: from a letter by George Breeze, a convicted murderer of 1904; chapter 24: 'The Times They Are A-changing' by Bob Dylan; chapter 25: suffragist song of 1907; chapter 26: 'The Men Who Make the Steel' by Ian Chesterman, from a 1973 record produced by the Shotton Steelworks Action Committee; chapter 29: words from a health poster, sung by Tony Hancock in the BBC TV programme 'The Blood Donor' (1961); chapter 30: 'Football Crazy', a popular song. The verses for chapters 22 and 26 are from 'A Ballad History of England' by Roy Palmer (Batsford, 1979).

In a few cases, I have been unable to trace the sources of written evidence and would like to apologise to anyone who has therefore been omitted from the following list. Written sources used are as follows (page numbers are given first): 7B: Marchioness Curzon of Keddleston: *Memoirs* (Hutchinson, 1955); 7C: Nicolson: *Small Talk* (Constable, 1937); 8B & 8C: S Rowntree: *Poverty: A Study of Town Life* (1901); 9E: Lady Bell: *At the Works: A Study of a Manufacturing Town* (Edward Arnold, 1907); 9F: *Agricultural Labourers' Wages, Earnings*, etc. Cd. 2376 (1905); 10A: Government paper (1909); 13C: *Lloyds Weekly News* (April 1912); 13E: *TV Times* (1983); 17A: Harold Macmillan: *The Winds of Change;* 17C: Agatha Christie: *An Autobiography* (Wm Collins, 1977); 19D: *Daily Mirror* (July 1st 1976); 19E: *War Letters of Fallen Englishmen* (Victor Gollancz); 21C: Graham Greene: *A Sort of Life* (Bodley Head, 1971); 23C: *Observer* Magazine, New British series; 25D: Marie Stopes: *Mother England – a Contemporary History* (John Bale, 1929); 27C: L Baily: *BBC Scrapbook*, volume 2 (Allen & Unwin, 1968); 29B: H L Beales and R S Lambert: *Memoirs of the Unemployed* (Gollancz, 1934); 29C: quoted in L C B Seaman: *Life in Britain between the Wars*

Agatha Christie in 1932.

(Batsford, 1970); 40A: Robert Graves & Alan Hodge: *The Long Weekend* (Faber & Faber, 1941); 41E: quoted in Branson & Heinemann: *Britain in the 1930s* (Weidenfeld & Nicholson, 1971); 43B: BBC radio broadcast (1984); 45B B Kops: *The World is a Wedding* (1963); 45D: T.L.S. (14.9.40); 47B: M.O.I. film: *Dawn Guard* (1941); 47C: H Nicolson: *Diaries and Letters*, 1939-45, edited by N Nicolson (Collins, 1967); 49E: BBC news bulletin (8.1.85); 51B: R C Robertson-Glasgow in the *Sunday Times*; 51C: P Jennings in the *Telegraph* colour magazine; 55A: C Chaplin: *My Autobiography* (Bodley Head, 1964); 55B: R Dahl: *Boy* (Cape); 57E: Enoch Powell, quoted in *The Day Before Yesterday* (Sidgwick & Jackson/Thames TV, 1971); 59E: The Sydney *Sun*; 59F: BBC2 interview; 59G: quoted in T Palmer: *All You Need is Love* (Weidenfeld & Nicholson, 1976); 61A: *The Times*; 61B and 61F: *Radio Times 50th Anniversary Souvenir* (1973); 61D: *BBC Handbook* (1962); 61E *BBC Handbook* (1984); 63: Diary quoted in *Binham – A Social Survey 1942-43* (W.E.A. Eastern District); 67C: *Radio Times* (4.8.84); 67D: James Cameron: *Point of Departure* (A Barker, 1967); 69C: *Police Chronicle* (26.4.18); 71C: *Observer* New British series; 71D: BBC radio 4; 73B: F Sherwood Taylor: *The Century of Science* (Heinemann, 1940); 75A: As 9E; 75C: *The Sunday Times* (15.7.84); 75D: Mrs J G Frazer: *First Aid to the Servantless* (Wm Heffer, 1913); 81A: *Daily Telegraph* (20.8.69); 81E: BBC TV news (August 1984); 87B: MORI survey for *Now!* magazine (14.9.79); 87C: *Picture Post* (13.7.46); 89B: Channel 4 TV programme; 92: *The Times* (24.1.85).

Glossary

abortion – deliberate ending of a pregnancy to prevent a baby being born

affluent – rich

air-raid warden – person employed to check on buildings and people during and after a raid

alliance – an agreement between countries

Anderson shelter – garden shelter for use during air raids

armistice – a stop in the fighting

assassinated – killed

assembly line – a system for making goods in a factory; the product is put together stage by stage

atom bomb – bomb which uses the power released when atoms are split; causes **radiation** and a vast amount of destruction

attrition – gradually wearing down

automation – automatic control of the process of making a product

bankrupt – unable to pay debts; without money

barrage balloon – a barrier against air attack

birched – beaten with a stick

blackout – turning off or covering all lights

Blitz – a sudden air attack

capital punishment – the death sentence for crimes

censored – changed, usually by missing out something

chalet – a holiday home

chaperone – woman who accompanies single woman in public

civil servant – a person employed by the government

civil war – a war between people of the same country

coalition – a government made up of more than one party

cocktail – an alcoholic mixed drink

colony – land governed by another country

commission – group of people chosen by the government to do a special job

commute – travel some distance daily from home to work

consciousness – being aware

conscription – situation in which people are made to join the forces

consumer society – people who buy goods to satisfy needs and desires

contraception – a way of avoiding becoming pregnant

council house – a house built by a council and rented

depression – a period when trade is bad

dialysis – a process involving separation of substances

dictator – a person with complete power over others

diphtheria – a dangerous throat disease

dreadnought – a big battleship, with heavy armour

elementary school – a school like a primary school

emancipation – freedom

evacuated – taken from somewhere to go somewhere safer

executive – the people who carry out the laws

fatal – causing death

flapper – a young girl of the 1920s who enjoyed life

governess – a woman who teaches children privately

grammar school – a school in which Latin was taught

hippies – people who reject society's standards in favour of living more freely

hire purchase – a way of buying something by a number of payments spread over some time

hunger-strike – not eating as a way of protesting

hydrogen bomb – similar to the atom bomb, but more powerful

infantry – soldiers who fight on foot

invested – put money into something to make a profit

jazz – a style of American music

kidney machine – one which does the job of human kidneys

lentil – a vegetable like a small bean

listing – tipping to one side

Luftwaffe – the German air force

malnutrition – condition caused by lack of the right food

manifesto – a statement of what the party will do if it is elected

martyr – a person who would die for his/her beliefs

mass-producing – making goods in huge numbers

matron – a woman in charge of the nursing in a hospital

microchip – a tiny object which forms the 'works' of electronic goods, such as computers

middle class – people between the upper and working classes, such as doctors, lawyers, etc.

militant – fighting

minority – a small group

mobilised – got ready for war

mortgage – money borrowed to buy a house which is paid back over a number of years

munitions – materials used in war (e.g. shells)

National Insurance – a system organised by the government to insure people against sickness, etc.

nuclear war – a war involving atomic weapons

obese – very fat indeed

on the parish – getting money from the local poor rates

open prison – 'prisons without bars', for trusted prisoners

parasol – an umbrella to protect against the sun

patriotic – loving one's own country

pauper – a person without any income

pawnbroker – a man who lends money to people who leave their possessions at his shop

penalised – punished

petition – a request, signed by many people

picketing – trying to persuade people not to work

polio – a disease which can paralyse people

prescription – written order for medicine

probation – a system of allowing the criminals to go free without punishment, unless they commit another crime

productivity – the power and ability to make goods

prophecies – statements about what is going to happen

prosperity – wealth and success

Protestant – a Christian who does not belong to the Roman Catholic (or Greek) church

radiation – dangerous rays given out when atom bombs explode

radioactive – having rays which can cause radiation sickness

rationing – allowing people a fixed amount of some item which is in short supply

recession – a slight decline in trade

renal – to do with the kidneys

republic – a country without a king or queen

rural – in the country

shareholder – a person who has bought shares in a company, hoping to make a profit

Sinn Fein – a party begun in 1905 to win independence for Ireland; the name means 'ourselves alone'

slum – a dirty, overcrowded building or area

slump – a bad or sudden drop in trade

sniper – a person who shoots at individual soldiers

spats – short ankle-coverings

squalor – dirt and misery

Stuka – a German dive-bomber

supersonic – faster than the speed of sound

surrogate – substitute

tetanus – a disease which makes the muscles move violently

transistor – a small electronic object used instead of a valve

treason – a crime against the king, queen or country

'trench foot' – a foot disease, caused by standing in the cold and wet

typhoid – a fever caused by food or drink having germs in it

ultimatum – a final demand, including a threat of what will happen if it is not met

white feather – a sign of cowardice

workhouse – where fit poor people had to live and work

zeppelin – an airship

Index